# GREAT BOWLS OF FIRE!

# Great
# Bowls
# of Fire!

## Dave DeWitt and W.C. Longacre

PHOTOGRAPHY BY
### Lois Ellen Frank

Ten Speed Press
Berkeley, California

1🖘
Ten Speed Press
Post Office Box 7123
Berkeley, California 94707

Distributed in Australia by Simon & Schuster Australia,
in Canada by Publishers Group West, in New Zealand by
Tandem Press, in South Africa by Real Books, in the United
Kingdom and Europe by Airlift Books, and in Malaysia,
Singapore, and Indonesia by Berkeley Books.

Cover design by Fifth Street Design
Text design by Nadja Lazansky

Library of Congress Cataloging-in-Publication Data:
Dewitt, Dave.
    Great bowls of fire!/Dave Dewitt and W.C. Longacre;
photography by Lois Ellen Frank.
        p. cm.
    Includes index.
    ISBN 0-89815-901-6
    1. Soups. 2. Cookery (Hot peppers) 3. Spices. I. Longacre.
W.C. II. Title
TX757.D488 1997
641.8'13--dc21                                    97-25881
                                                  CIP

First printing, 1997
Printed in Canada
1 2 3 4 5 6 7 8 9 10—01 00 99 98 97

# Contents

ACKNOWLEDGMENTS

*Thanks to all the fine folks*
*who helped out with this book:*
*Margarita, Sue Baylor, Martha Doster,*
*Chef Robert Lloyd,*
*Dale Wagy (our fishing guide),*
*and Mary Jane Wilan.*

# Introduction:
# A Spicy Pair of
# Soupiers at Play

Soups are the elegant side of a chef's kitchen. In professional cooking, tradition holds that the head chef often insists on making the soup. In fact, if you catch the chef eating something in his kitchen, chances are it will be a soup. Why do chefs love soups? Because it gives them a chance to recycle some of the by-products of the main dishes, as well as take advantage of seasonal ingredients. Chefs believe that soups are the everyday practice of the art of balancing flavors, and the same concepts used to make great sauces will work to make great soups. Soup-making is an elegant art and an understated way to show off one's culinary expertise.

Chefs also love soups because they are make-ahead meals that can be held for a long time before serving. A soup to open a meal signals that what follows will be an elegant feast. Yet soups are also basic comfort foods and can become a full meal when served with the right accompaniments. Also, soups are a great way to use up supermarket loss leaders or special sales. For example, salmon does not freeze particularly well, but salmon stock does.

We consider ourselves to be soupiers, an invented term for chefs who specialize in soup-making much like a saucier specializes in preparing sauces. But W.C. is the real chef of the pair and created most of the recipes in this book. He started focusing on soups in 1976 at his first restaurant, the Morning Glory Cafe in Albuquerque, where he featured a freshly made soup of the day. He experimented with hundreds of soups—most were bowls of fire—as he tested them with his customers over the years. In subsequent cooking stints in Hong Kong and Key West, he experimented with

Asian and Caribbean soups. During his years as chef and owner of the Portside Restaurant in Key West, he learned the techniques of seafood soups and chowders with quite a kick from the habanero and Scotch bonnet chiles that were available in Key West markets.

These days at W.C.'s Mountain Road Cafe in Albuquerque, he prepares three hot and spicy soup specials every day, and soup lovers can feast on a sampler of smaller bowls of fire that, with his special red chile bread, make a filling meal. W.C. was the first winner of the Albuquerque Souper Bowl, a competition held the Saturday before the Super Bowl in January. It began in 1995 as a event for the Roadrunner Food Bank to benefit the homeless and was held at Wild Oats Market. About fifteen top chefs from New Mexico enter their best soups and are judged by the general public, who pay to taste them all. W.C. has won the Souper Bowl twice and finished second once.

Dave's connection to these bowls of fire comes from his annual chile garden. Since he is an avid chile grower, he constantly experiments with growing seed from exotic varieties. Inevitably, he has a bumper crop and is continually passing them on to W.C. so that he can invent soups with new flavors. There are some exotic chiles in the recipes in this book, but we provide substitutions of readily available chiles. Dave also collected soup recipes on his travels around the world researching chile pepper lore; many of those recipes are included in this book.

We should mention the fact that some of the recipes here serve small numbers of people, while others are designed to serve ten to twelve. In most cases, the smaller servings are for fragile soups that do not freeze particularly well. Thus the larger-yielding recipes are designed for freezing and later serving. It is just as much trouble to make 2 gallons as 2 quarts of soup, assuming that the cook has the freezer space to store it. Soups in the freezer are a great backup if unexpected company shows up or if the household cook doesn't feel very creative at the moment. A frozen supply of these great bowls of fire are perfect to take to neighbors, to give as gifts, or to help those suffering from illnesses.

A note on the heat scale. We've used the same mild, medium, hot, and extremely hot ratings for the recipes that we've used for years now. They are based on our own tastes, taking into consideration the type of chile in the recipe, the amount of it used, and its dilution with other ingredients. Cooks who wish to increase or decrease heat levels based on these ratings can easily adjust the amount of chile in them.

## DEFINITIONS

The following are our definitions of the styles of soup prepared in this book:

BISQUE: A thick soup often consisting of puréed seafood, fowl, or vegetables and cream, milk, or a white sauce.

BROTH OR BOUILLON: The liquid from cooking meat, vegetables, or fish in water.

CHILI: A thick stew of meat, chile peppers, spices, and sometimes other ingredients.

CHOWDER: A chunky and thick seafood soup.

CONSOMMÉ: A clarified meat, fish, or vegetable broth that is served hot or cold.

GUMBO: A thick Creole soup or stew thickened with okra or filé (sassafras leaves) that is begun by making a roux.

STEW: Any dish prepared by stewing, but usually meaning a dish with meat and/or vegetables in a broth.

# Tools of the Spicy–Soup Trade

We suggest that anyone interested in becoming a soupier invest in a good stockpot with a capacity of at least ten quarts. It is by far the best pot for making large quantities of soups or stews. Other pots can be used, including Dutch ovens. A "china cap" is better than a standard sieve or colander for straining. It is a conical, perforated stainless steel sieve with a handle and a bracket so it can hang on the stockpot. It can also be used to remove the skins and seeds from tomatoes. By lining the china cap with cheesecloth during straining, the cook can make a clear broth.

There are several essential tools for grinding, chopping, and puréeing. An electric spice mill is perfect for grinding chiles and spices into powder, but a spice-dedicated coffee grinder will also work. A small blender or mini-chopper works well for small amounts of garlic or onion that need to be minced. A food processor is a necessity for heavy-duty chopping and grating, but a large commercial blender is better for puréeing.

The apprentice soupier will need two whisks, one long and one short, one made of rigid wire, one of piano wire. Buy these at a restaurant supply store. Measuring spoons on a ring are handy because the cook won't have to interrupt preparing the soup to search the drawer for the one-fourth teaspoon. Pyrex measuring cups are essential—buy two or three of every size; some soups have both wet and dry ingredients, and this quantity will save the cook from washing and drying cups when he or she should be concentrating on making the recipe.

A variable-grind pepper mill insures that the proper grind of pepper will make it to the soup. Another handy tool is a stainless steel box grater; we recommend buying a large one since the smaller ones bend too easily. A slotted spoon is a necessity for adding ingredients to the soup without splashing or for removing things from the soup. An "Asian spider" can be used for the same task; it is wire mesh on a wooden handle. A double boiler is used to hold cream soups at a constant temperature before serving, or for warming any soup that can't be boiled. For sautéing, several sizes of heavy skillets will be needed, including a cast-iron skillet. Woks are multipurpose devices used to steam, boil, sear, and stir-fry. An unusual skillet is a ribbed cast-iron skillet with ribs about one inch apart. It is an ideal substitute for grilling if an open flame is not available. It will keep the meat out of its own fats and juices.

Also important in the soup kitchen is good cutlery for chopping and mincing. Cleavers are very handy, and inexpensive ones can be found at Asian markets. The heavier ones work better. Cleavers are actually safer to use than knives. An essential tool is a large, heavy wooden cutting board.

Finally, we believe that gas stoves are better for making soups than electric ones because the temperature can be more precisely controlled.

# I.
# Soup-making Essentials

In this chapter we present some essential recipes for making the soups and stews in this book. By far, stocks are the most important ingredients for creating great bowls of fire.

## MAKING GOOD STOCKS

It is an axiom of soup-making that a great soup starts with a great stock. So, if a cook is going to go to all the trouble of making a soup from scratch, first make a good stock. It doesn't take very much time to make good stocks, and in many cases they are the keys to the vibrant flavors of the soups in this book. Stocks store well and freeze well, so they are worth the effort it takes to make them.

To make a good stock, use real ingredients—do not use bouillon cubes or powders, or canned stocks. Use fresh garlic (not granulated) and fresh celery leaves. Always use fresh herbs unless they are unavailable; if using dry herbs, double the amount in the recipe.

W.C. says that the trash can or garbage disposal is the enemy of a good stock. He tries to recycle as much as he can in the kitchen. He points out that in professional chef competitions, the trash is weighed and chefs have points deducted for disposing of too much. W.C. keeps several plastic bags in the freezer of trimmed and leftover ingredients that can be used in stocks. He saves such things as the end pieces of onions and carrots, and the trimmings from celery, parsley stems, and mushroom stems. He saves bones for meat stocks, and fish parts, bones, trimmings, and shrimp shells for seafood stocks. Sometimes seafood markets and butchers can be talked out of their trimmings, and you can turn them into great stocks.

Stocks should be concentrated, so be sure to boil them down. This is a classic French reduction technique, and the cook can always add the water back to the concentrated stock. Soups will taste better using concentrated stocks, and they take up less room in the freezer.

After the stock has been reduced, cool it in the freezer; any fat will rise to the top and congeal, and it can be removed with a spoon. Instead of using bouillon cubes, freeze the stock in ice cube trays and store the cubes in zip bags. Then you can have small amounts of stock when you need them.

# Red Thai Curry Paste

If fresh New Mexican red chiles are not available, rehydrate the dried red pods in hot water until they are soft, then drain them and use them as a substitute.

20 fresh New Mexican red chiles, seeded and stemmed
2 stalks lemongrass, thinly sliced
4 small shallots, thinly sliced
1 large clove garlic
1 tablespoon peeled, grated fresh ginger
Zest of ½ lime
¼ cup cilantro leaves
½ teaspoon ground coriander
½ teaspoon ground caraway
1 tablespoon Thai fish sauce
4 medium shrimp, peeled
2 tablespoons soy oil
½ tablespoon toasted sesame oil

Combine all ingredients in a food processor and process until smooth. It will keep in the refrigerator for two weeks.

Yield: 3 cups

# Jamaican Jerk Marinade

HEAT SCALE: EXTREMELY HOT

The number of versions of jerk marinades is nothing less than astonishing. Of course, every one of them is "authentic, secret, and the most flavorful"—as is this one. Traditionally, the marinade should be very thick and can be used with pork, chicken, or fish.

¼ cup whole Jamaican pimento berries (allspice)

3 habanero chiles, seeded, stemmed, and chopped

10 green onions, white and green parts, chopped

½ onion, chopped

4 cloves garlic, chopped

4 bay leaves, crushed

3 tablespoons peeled, chopped fresh ginger

⅓ cup fresh thyme

1 tablespoon freshly ground black pepper

1 teaspoon ground nutmeg

1 teaspoon ground cinnamon

1 teaspoon salt (or more to taste)

¼ cup fresh lime juice

¼ cup vegetable oil

Roast the berries in a dry skillet until they are aromatic, about 2 minutes. Remove them from the skillet and crush them to a powder in a mortar or spice mill.

Place the powder and the remaining ingredients in a food processor and process to make a paste or sauce. Adjust the consistency with a little more lime juice or water. Stored in the refrigerator, it will keep for a month or more.

YIELD: 2½ TO 3 CUPS

# Rouille Hot Sauce

The famous food writer M.F.K. Fisher described this French sauce as "a peppery concoction suited to the taste of *bouillabaisse*, served separately from the soup to be ladled in at the discretion of the individual diner." When you taste it, you won't limit its use to just one soup.

2 small red bell peppers, seeded, stemmed, and cut in small squares

2 small, hot dried chiles, such as piquin or Thai, crushed

1 cup water

2 whole canned or bottled pimientos, drained, dried, and coarsely chopped (optional)

4 cloves garlic, coarsely chopped

6 tablespoons olive oil

1 to 3 teaspoons fine dry bread crumbs

Salt to taste

In a saucepan, combine the bell peppers, dried chiles, and water. Simmer until the peppers are soft, then drain the peppers and pat dry. Place the peppers, pimientos, and garlic in a mixing bowl or mortar and mash the ingredients together to make a smooth paste. Slowly beat in the olive oil and bread crumbs until the mixture becomes just too thick to pour. Or, place the peppers, pimientos, and garlic in a blender and purée while adding the olive oil and bread crumbs. Then add salt to taste.

YIELD: ABOUT 1 CUP

# Berbere Paste

Originally used as the sauce for *kifto* (fresh raw meat dishes), berbere is now used as both an ingredient and a condiment in Ethiopian cooking. Like *harissa*, it is essentially a curry paste with an abundance of red chiles. Serve sparingly as a condiment with grilled meats and poultry or add to soups and stews. This paste will keep for a couple of months under refrigeration.

1 teaspoon ground cardamom

2 teaspoons cumin seeds

½ teaspoon coriander seeds

¼ teaspoon ground cinnamon

½ teaspoon black peppercorns

½ teaspoon fenugreek seeds

1 small onion, coarsely chopped

4 cloves garlic

1 cup water

14 dried piquin chiles, stems removed

1 tablespoon cayenne

2 tablespoons paprika

½ teaspoon ground ginger

¼ teaspoon ground allspice

¼ teaspoon ground nutmeg

¼ teaspoon ground cloves

3 tablespoons dry red wine

3 tablespoons vegetable oil

Toast the cardamom, cumin, coriander, cinnamon, peppercorns, and fenugreek in a hot skillet, shaking constantly, for a couple of minutes, until they start to toast and become aromatic. In a spice mill, grind these spices into a powder.

Combine the onion, garlic, and ½ cup of the water in a blender or food processor and purée until smooth. Add the roasted spice powder, piquins, cayenne, paprika, ginger, allspice, nutmeg, and cloves and continue to blend. Slowly add the remaining ½ cup water, wine, and oil and blend until smooth. Place the sauce in a small saucepan and simmer for 15 minutes to blend the flavors and thicken.

YIELD: ABOUT 1 CUP

# Ethiopian Curried Butter

HEAT SCALE: MILD

Known as *nit'ir qibe*, this interesting butter oil is a basic ingredient in the preparation of traditional Ethiopian foods. Since it is made from clarified butter, it will last for months in a glass jar in the refrigerator.

1 (3-inch) piece fresh ginger, peeled and grated
½ cup minced onion
1 clove garlic, minced
4 cups (2 pounds) butter
1 stick cinnamon
1 tablespoon fenugreek seeds
2 teaspoons cumin seeds
1 tablespoon minced fresh basil
1 teaspoon cardamom seeds
1 tablespoon minced fresh oregano

½ teaspoon turmeric powder

¼ teaspoon ground nutmeg

2 whole cloves

Combine the ginger, onion, and garlic in a mortar and pound to a coarse paste. Set aside.

In a medium saucepan, melt the butter over low heat, stirring constantly, taking care that the butter does not darken. Skim off the foam as it rises, and continue cooking and skimming until all the foam is gone.

Add the paste and the remaining ingredients to the butter and simmer, uncovered, at the lowest possible heat, stirring occasionally, for 30 minutes.

Remove from the heat and allow to cool. Pour off the transparent top layer of butter, leaving as much of the milk solids and spices as possible in the bottom of the saucepan. Discard the solids. Strain the butter through several layers of cheesecloth. The butter will usually be a liquid at room temperature and solidify in the refrigerator, where it can be kept, covered, for 3 or 4 months.

YIELD: ABOUT 2 CUPS

# Basic Beef Stock

The time invested in this procedure will pay off big in the recipes that follow, and as an additional bonus you'll find dogs hanging around your kitchen! This stock will keep for about a week in the refrigerator, and will keep in the freezer for months. The yield will depend on how much reduction occurs during the cooking. W.C. has been known to work with a stock for 100 hours, constantly adding water and reducing. Here we have described a minimum reduction time.

½ cup (4 ounces) butter
1½ pounds stew beef
3 marrow bones
½ cup red wine
1 tablespoon salt
1 bunch parsley, washed
2 small carrots, unpeeled, quartered
½ teaspoon thyme
1½ tablespoons black peppercorns
2 medium onions, quartered
¼ teaspoon cloves
2 small leeks, cut in ½-inch pieces
3 large bay leaves
2 celery stalks, including leaves and heart
1 turnip, quartered (optional)
8 quarts water

In a shallow glass baking dish, melt the butter. Place the meat and bones on top of the butter and pour the wine over all. Cover with foil and bake at 375° for 30 minutes. Transfer the meat from the dish (including all the scrapings) to a stockpot.

Add the remaining ingredients and bring to a boil. Reduce the heat, skim any foam off the top and simmer, uncovered, for 2 hours. Remove from the heat and strain through cheesecloth. Refrigerate or freeze and discard the fat that rises to the top.

YIELD: 6 QUARTS

# Mountain Road Cafe
# Classic Chicken Stock

This stock is the basis of many of the soups in this book. It's a flavorful classic stock from the French school and may be reduced further to intensify the flavor. It freezes very well. In addition, the poached chicken may be used in other recipes in this book. If you've been buying bouillon in cubes or cans, do yourself a favor and make this stock from scratch.

1 (4- to 5-pound) roasting hen, free-range if possible
1 gallon water
½ tablespoon salt
4 whole bay leaves
1 medium onion, cut in half
4 cloves garlic
1 bunch parsley, washed
1½ teaspoons peppercorns
1 large carrot, cut in half
1 celery stalk, including leaves

To prepare the chicken, set the hen on a cutting board. With the flat side of a cleaver, press down on the breast until you hear the bone break. Turn on its side and with the dull side of the cleaver, hit the drumstick at the midpoint one time with enough force to crack the bone. Do the same to the wing. Turn the hen on the other side and repeat. Turn the hen with the breast down and strike the back bone perpendicularly twice, each about a third of the way in from each side, to crack the back. (Breaking the chicken bones releases marrow into the stock, which adds more flavor.)

In a large stockpot, combine the water, salt, bay leaves, onion, garlic, parsley, peppercorns, carrot, and celery and bring to a boil. Add the chicken and boil, uncovered, for 1 to 1½ hours, adding more water to keep the chicken covered. Skim off any foam that rises.

To test the chicken for doneness, pull on one of the legs. It should separate without force at the joint and there should not be any visible blood. Do not overcook the chicken.

Remove the chicken and save for another use. Strain the stock and reserve. For a clearer stock, line the strainer with cheesecloth. Chill the stock in the freezer until the fat congeals, then remove it with a spoon.

YIELD: ABOUT 1 GALLON

# Wonton Soup Broth

This broth is a key ingredient for the wonton soups in this book. Chileheads who require pungency, other than from the wontons, can add five or six whole chile pods such as santaka or piquin. Remove them before serving.

3½ quarts Vibrant Vegetable Stock (page 19) or Mountain
   Road Cafe Classic Chicken Stock (page 15)
2 teaspoons ground ginger
1 teaspoon five-spice powder
2 teaspoons sugar
1 tablespoon hoisin sauce
2 tablespoons Chinese rice wine
1 cup ⅛-inch-long pieces of green onions

Heat the stock in a large stockpot and add the ginger, five-spice powder, sugar, and hoisin sauce. Bring to a boil, then reduce the heat to medium, add the rice wine and the green onions, and cook for 5 minutes.

YIELD: 3½ QUARTS

# Traditional European Fish Stock

This is a basic recipe, so don't be afraid to embellish it. Any frozen seafood trimmings (such as shrimp shells) can be added, or any frozen fish from the fishing trip three years ago that you don't want to serve as an entrée. Rich fish like salmon make a better stock. Feel free to add fresh herbs from your garden, too. This keeps in the refrigerator for about a week and freezes well. (The difference between this and court bouillon is that the latter is used for poaching rather than as a base for stocks.)

2 pounds fish trimmings, such as bones, skin, heads, and tails (not entrails)
2 tablespoons butter
3 quarts water
¼ cup fresh parsley leaves, packed
2 medium onions, quartered
4 large whole bay leaves
6 large cloves garlic
2 tablespoons black peppercorns, bruised
1 large leek, white part only, cut into ¼-inch rounds
3 large celery stalks, including leaves and heart, chopped
3 small carrots, cut into ½-inch rings
2 teaspoons salt

In a large, heavy stockpot, sauté the fish trimmings in butter for 3 minutes. Add the water, bring to a boil, and add the remaining ingredients. Reduce the heat and simmer uncovered for 1 hour. Remove from the heat and strain through cheesecloth.

YIELD: APPROXIMATELY 2 QUARTS

# Vibrant Vegetable Stock

This stock is good enough to serve as a first course consommé, in addition to using it as a base for many of the recipes in this book. Baking or caramelizing the vegetables before adding the water gives an additional richness to the stock. If you wish, adding a 1- to 2-inch piece of kombu seaweed will also add a further depth of flavor. This stock will keep for 2 days, covered, in the refrigerator. It can also be frozen; divide it into 2- or 3-cup freezer containers. The jalapeños are optional for making the stock spicy. Feel free to add any vegetable trimmings from the bag in your freezer, but beware of cabbage or broccoli—those flavors tend to dominate the stock.

4 onions, unpeeled, cut into eighths

3 large celery stalks, cut into fourths

2 leeks, white part only, coarsely chopped

1 head garlic cloves, separated and peeled

4 unpeeled carrots, cut into 2-inch pieces

1½ cups dry white wine

2 tablespoons high-quality olive oil

3 green onions, cut into 1-inch pieces

⅓ cup chopped parsley, including the stems

¼ cup fresh chopped basil or 2 tablespoons of dried basil

1 teaspoon dried marjoram

½ cup chopped button mushrooms

½ cup chopped celery leaves

1 zucchini, peeled and sliced

3 cups coarsely chopped tomatoes

3 jalapeño chiles, seeded, stemmed, and chopped (optional)

3 quarts cold water

5 whole black peppercorns

Heat the oven to 350°. Place the onions, celery, leeks, garlic, and carrots in a shallow pan and pour the wine over the top. Bake uncovered for 1½ hours.

Heat the oil in a stock pot and add the caramelized vegetables and the green onions. Sauté for 5 minutes, stirring occasionally. Add the remaining ingredients (except the water and peppercorns) and sauté for 5 minutes, stirring occasionally.

Add the water and the peppercorns and bring the mixture to a boil. Then lower the heat to a simmer, cover, and cook for 2 hours. Remove the cover and simmer for another 30 minutes. Strain the stock through a fine strainer lined with cheesecloth or a coffee filter, and add salt to taste.

Yield: About 2½ quarts

# Wonton Pasta

For purists who don't want to buy prepared wonton skins, here's a recipe to make them.

⅛ teaspoon Hungarian hot paprika
1 tablespoon plus 1 teaspoon water
2 cups flour
2 medium eggs
2 medium egg whites
½ teaspoon salt
2 tablespoons peanut oil

In a glass, combine the paprika and the water, stir well and set aside. In a mixing bowl, combine the remaining ingredients, then add the paprika water and stir with a wooden spoon until well mixed, but don't overmix. Make a dough ball by hand kneading. When it is a smooth ball, cover with plastic wrap and let set for 30 minutes.

Roll the ball through a pasta machine at the thinnest setting, dusting with flour to prevent sticking. Cut into 3-inch squares and fill the squares with the filling as soon as possible. Or, wrap the wonton skins tightly in plastic wrap, keeping out as much air as possible.

YIELD: 40 TO 50 SKINS

# Dried Herb Croutons

These crispy garnishes for the soups in this book are easy to make. The flavorings can include, but are not limited to, granulated garlic, rosemary, thyme, oregano, ground ginger, chile powder, and five-spice powder. Let the style and country of origin of the soup you are preparing be your guide. Pulverize the dried herbs between your palms to release their fragrance.

Leftover bread or French baguettes
Vegetable oil for frying
Herbs and spices of choice

Cut the bread into small cubes and fry in the oil until brown, turning often. Drain on paper towels. Add to a paper bag with your favorite herbs and spices and shake well.

# 2.
# Sauces and Starters

## White Sauce #1

This is the richer of the two white sauces—a classic French béchamel. It will refrigerate well, but we caution when reheating it as it scorches easily. Use a double boiler and don't let this sauce come to a boil. You may adjust the thickness by adding a little more milk or cream.

1 cup (8 ounces) sweet butter
1¼ cups all-purpose flour
1½ cups scalded milk
1 quart heavy cream
¼ teaspoon white pepper
¼ teaspoon salt
⅛ teaspoon freshly ground nutmeg

Melt the butter in a stockpot over low heat. Whisk in the flour and heat until thickened to make a roux; do not brown. Whisk in the milk, and still whisking, add the heavy cream. Whisk until there are no lumps in the sauce. Cook until thickened and the "raw" taste of the flour is gone. Add the pepper, salt, and nutmeg, and mix well.

YIELD: 2 QUARTS

# White Sauce #2

This a mock béchamel that has less fat that White Sauce #1. You may wish to add a teaspoon of sugar to give the illusion of richness—after all, it's only seventeen calories. This sauce will last for a week in the refrigerator. Be sure to reheat it in a double boiler.

1 cup (8 ounces) margarine
1¼ cups all-purpose flour
6 cups scalded milk
¼ teaspoon white pepper
¼ teaspoon salt
⅛ teaspoon freshly ground nutmeg

Melt the margarine in a stockpot over low heat. Add the flour and stir with a whisk until thickened to make a roux. Do not brown. Slowly blend in the milk and whisk briskly until there are no lumps. Cook until thickened and the "raw" taste of the flour is gone. Add the pepper, salt, and nutmeg, and mix well.

YIELD: 2 QUARTS

# Piri-Piri Sauce

This sauce originated in Portugal and spread to Portuguese colonies in Africa and China. Note that this recipe requires advance preparation.

1 ½ cups small, hot dried chiles such as santaka or Thai, crumbled
¼ cup blended whiskey
⅛ cup extra virgin olive oil
⅛ cup canola oil

Combine all ingredients in a jar, cover tightly, and shake well. Let the sauce marinate for two weeks, shaking the jar every two days.

YIELD: ½ CUP

# W.C.'s Green Chile Sauce

Heat scale: Medium

This recipe dates to 1976, when W.C. created it for his first restaurant, the Morning Glory Cafe. It is meatless and dairyless and is easily frozen or canned.

6 cups chopped hot New Mexican green chiles, seeded and
    stemmed
1 clove garlic, minced
1 medium onion, coarsely chopped
⅛ teaspoon ground coriander
½ tablespoon red chile powder
½ teaspoon white pepper
½ teaspoon ground cumin
1 tablespoon salt
11½ cups water
2 tablespoons cornstarch

In a large stockpot, combine the green chiles, garlic, onion, coriander, red chile powder, white pepper, cumin, salt, and 10 cups of water. Bring to a boil and boil, uncovered, for 1 hour.

In a small bowl, combine the cornstarch and 1½ cups of water and mix thoroughly. Add to the chile mixture and cook until the mixture clears, about 20 minutes.

Yield: About 12 cups

# Sweet and Hot Pepper Consommé

The flavor of peppers dominates this powerful, spiced-up broth. This recipe can also be used as a vegetarian stock for making other soups and stews. It is an elegant example of a first-course soup that may precede any spicy entrée.

4 red bell peppers, quartered

4 green bell peppers, quartered

6 large ripe tomatoes, quartered

2 large onions, quartered

2 large hot New Mexican green chiles, split, seeded, and stemmed

3 whole bay leaves

3 large jalapeño chiles, split, seeded, and stemmed

½ cup chopped fresh parsley

2 whole cloves

3 large cloves garlic

1 ½ tablespoons salt

6 quarts boiling Vibrant Vegetable Stock (page 19)

In a large stockpot, stir together all ingredients except the stock. Pour the boiling stock over the ingredients and boil for 10 minutes. Reduce the heat and simmer, covered, for 1 ½ hours.

Remove from the heat and cool. Strain through a fine sieve. Serve hot or cold.

SERVES: 10 TO 12

# Tomato-Orange Ginger Soup

HEAT SCALE: VARIES

This is an exciting blend of fresh, light flavors that makes a great beginning-of-the-meal palate stimulator during the summer. It has beautiful color and a slight bite from the ginger. A thinly sliced lime round makes an excellent garnish when floated on the soup with a dollop of sour cream on the top.

2 medium onions, finely chopped

3 cloves garlic, finely chopped

4 tablespoons sweet butter

Zest of ½ orange

6 cups puréed fresh tomatoes

1 (5-ounce) can tomato paste

6 cups freshly squeezed orange juice

1 teaspoon ground ginger

1 tablespoon finely grated fresh ginger

¼ teaspoon white pepper

½ teaspoon salt

¾ tablespoon sugar

Cayenne to taste

Sauté the onion and garlic in the butter over low heat, taking care not to brown. Add the zest and stir well. Transfer to a large stock-pot, add the remaining ingredients, and stir well. Bring just to a boil, lower the heat, and simmer for 15 minutes. Serve hot or allow to cool before serving.

SERVES: 8

# W.C.'s Chimayo Red Chile Sauce

This red chile sauce is also a soup—it is eaten in bowls or ladled over burritos, enchiladas, and other New Mexican entrées. The key is the rich, high-impact chicken stock that is made in the style of classic French poaching stocks, with plenty of herbs. W.C. uses Chimayo chile in this recipe, a flavorful variety from northern New Mexico with a brilliant red-orange color. He also uses a secret ingredient— a little chocolate—that has its origins in the mole sauces of central Mexico.

¼ cup vegetable oil (soy preferred)

5 cloves garlic, peeled

1 medium onion, chopped

½ tablespoon dried thyme

⅓ ounce unsweetened chocolate, coarsely chopped

1 tablespoon salt

1½ pounds ground red New Mexican chile (Chimayo preferred)

1 gallon Mountain Road Cafe Classic Chicken Stock (page 15)

1 quart water

In a food processor, combine the oil, garlic, onion, thyme, chocolate, and salt and purée to a coarse paste. Transfer to a bowl, add the ground red chile and mix.

In a large stockpot, heat the chicken stock to boiling. Add the paste and boil for 10 minutes, stirring occasionally. Add the water and boil for 5 minutes, or longer, until reaching the desired consistency, stirring constantly.

YIELD: ABOUT 1 GALLON

# Bahamian Pumpkin Habanero Cream Soup

     HEAT SCALE: HOT

This smooth bisque with island flavors has considerable heat and great color. Garnish it with fresh coconut shavings and serve it before a seafood entrée.

1 large onion, minced

¼ pound butter

2 tablespoons flour

2½ cups milk

½ cup cream

3 cups Vibrant Vegetable Stock (page 19) or Mountain Road Cafe Classic Chicken Stock (page 15)

3 cups cooked, mashed pumpkin

1 teaspoon salt

⅓ cup freshly squeezed lime juice

1 habanero chile, seeded, stemmed, and minced

¼ cup dark brown sugar

½ teaspoon ground ginger

½ teaspoon ground cinnamon

½ teaspoon ground mace

Shaved or grated fresh coconut, for garnish

In a stockpot, sauté the onion in the butter over medium heat until soft, about 5 minutes. Add the flour and stir until smooth, then add the milk and cream, stirring well. Slowly mix in the stock and pumpkin. Stir well and add the remaining ingredients. Reduce the heat and simmer for 10 minutes. Garnish with the coconut and serve.

SERVES: 6

# Posole with Red and Green Chile Sauces

HEAT SCALE: MEDIUM     ❦ ❦

This is our version of a classic corn and chile dish from northern New Mexico. Serving the chile sauces as side dishes instead of mixing them with the posole allows guests to adjust the heat to their own liking. Note that if you are using dry posole corn, this recipe requires advance preparation.

2 dried red New Mexican chiles, seeded and stemmed
8 ounces frozen posole corn, thawed, or dry posole corn that has been soaked in water overnight
1 teaspoon garlic powder
1 medium onion, chopped
6 cups Mountain Road Cafe Classic Chicken Stock (page 15)
1 pound pork loin, cut into 1-inch cubes
½ cup W.C.'s Green Chile Sauce (page 26)
½ cup W.C.'s Chimayo Red Chile Sauce (page 29)
Chopped fresh cilantro for garnish
Chopped onion for garnish

Combine the chiles, posole corn, garlic, onion, and chicken stock in a stockpot and boil for about 3 hours, or until the posole is tender, adding more water as needed.

Add the pork and continue cooking for ½ hour, or until the pork is tender but not falling apart. The result should resemble a soup more than a stew. Remove the chile pods.

Warm the green chile sauce and the red chile sauce and serve in small bowls for each guest to add to the posole. Serve the posole garnished with the cilantro and onion.

SERVES: 4

# Gulf of Mexico Seafood Tortilla Soup

 HEAT SCALE: MEDIUM

This soup was inspired by W.C.'s visits to Veracruz, Mexico, and its flavors are classic to the region. It's also very visually appealing, especially when you use large shrimp. This rich but fresh-tasting soup goes well with grilled entrées, so it's a great starter for a barbecue.

1 tablespoon olive oil

4 medium tomatoes, peeled, seeded, and coarsely chopped

6 green onions, green and white parts, chopped

1 tablespoon minced garlic

⅛ teaspoon ground bay leaf

4 cups Mountain Road Cafe Classic Chicken Stock (page 15) or Vibrant Vegetable Stock (page 19)

2 cups Traditional European Fish Stock (page 18)

1 teaspoon cayenne

½ teaspoon white pepper

¾ teaspoon salt

½ teaspoon minced fresh parsley

1 pound crab meat

1 pound medium shrimp, peeled and sliced into ¼-inch pieces

1 pound skinless red snapper fillets, cut into ½-inch pieces

¼ cup finely chopped red bell pepper

¼ cup finely chopped green bell pepper

¼ cup finely chopped yellow bell pepper

12 yellow corn tortillas

2 tablespoons vegetable shortening

1¼ pounds mozzarella cheese, grated

2½ tablespoons sugar

2 tablespoons freshly squeezed lemon juice

Heat the olive oil in a skillet and add the tomatoes, green onions, garlic, and bay leaf. Sauté for 10 minutes, stirring well. Remove from the heat and set aside.

In a stockpot, combine the stocks, cayenne, white pepper, salt, and parsley. Bring to a boil, reduce the heat, and simmer, uncovered, for 5 minutes. Add the sautéed tomatoes and mix well. Simmer for an additional 10 minutes. Add the crab meat, shrimp, red snapper, and bell peppers and simmer for an additional 10 minutes.

Cut the tortillas into strips ¼ inch by 2 inches. Heat the short-ening in a skillet and fry the strips until crisp. Remove and drain on paper towels.

Line 10 to 12 soup bowls with the tortilla strips and divide the cheese, sugar, and lemon juice among the bowls. Ladle in the soup, taking care to divide the seafood evenly.

SERVES: 10 TO 12

# Creamy Green Chile and
# Bay Shrimp Chowder

HEAT SCALE: MILD

This soup started as a seafood sauce for enchiladas, but the staff at the Mountain Road Cafe couldn't keep their spoons out of it, so W.C. turned it into a soup. It's very rich and hearty and can be garnished with fresh cilantro and a squeeze of lime.

1½ cups W.C.'s Green Chile Sauce (page 26)

3 cups Mountain Road Cafe Classic Chicken Stock (page 15)
   or Vibrant Vegetable Stock (page 19)

1 cup Traditional European Fish Stock (page 18)

3 cups White Sauce #1 or #2 (pages 23-24)

1 cup peas, fresh or frozen

2 cups potatoes, peeled and cut into ½-inch cubes

1 medium onion, chopped

2 tablespoons minced garlic

1 teaspoon chopped fresh thyme

¾ teaspoon chopped fresh basil

1 pound bay shrimp

1 cup milk

In a stockpot, combine the green chile sauce, chicken stock, and fish stock and heat to a simmer. Blend in the white sauce by whipping vigorously. Add the remaining ingredients except the milk and simmer for 15 minutes. Add the milk slowly, stirring constantly to avoid burning. Serve hot, garnished with croutons.

SERVES: 6

# 3.
# Blistering Bisques and Cream Soups

## Wild Mushroom Bisque with Grilled Chicken

HEAT SCALE: MILD

Every year on the Saturday preceding the Super Bowl, Wild Oats Market in Albuquerque sponsors the Chef's Invitational Souper Bowl Soup Contest. In 1995, W.C. defeated a dozen other Albuquerque chefs with this grand prize winner. Use whatever wild mushrooms you have to make 9 ounces—we have suggested a mixture below. W.C. gathered most of the mushrooms from the Sandia Mountains near Albuquerque and urges aficionados to learn about wild mushrooms.

1¾ pounds chicken breasts
½ cup teriyaki sauce
1½ tablespoons grated ginger
9 ounces mixed wild mushrooms (suggested: 2½ ounces boletes, 2½ ounces cèpes, 2 ounces morels, 1 ounce golden trumpets, 1 ounce black trumpets)
2 large shallots, minced
1 teaspoon minced garlic
1 teaspoon freshly ground black pepper
4 quarts Mountain Road Cafe Classic Chicken Stock (page 15)

½ medium onion, finely chopped

¾ cup butter, divided in thirds

1 pound domestic mushrooms, sliced

1 tablespoon minced garlic

¾ cup all-purpose flour

2 ounces hard Romano cheese, finely grated

1 quart cream

½ cup dry sherry

2 cups V-8 Juice

Salt to taste

Marinate the chicken in the teriyaki sauce and ginger for 20 minutes. Grill the chicken until done, chop fine, and set aside.

Soak the wild mushrooms in 3 cups warm water for 20 minutes. Rinse thoroughly and repeat soaking in 2 cups water. Remove the mushrooms from the water and chop fine. Reserve the water. Place the mushrooms, reserved water, shallots, garlic, black pepper, and chicken stock in a stockpot and boil for 30 minutes, adding water to maintain the original volume.

Sauté the onion in the ¼ cup butter and set aside.

Sauté the domestic mushrooms in ¼ cup butter with the garlic. Add the sautéed onions, mushrooms, and garlic to the stockpot.

Melt the remaining ¼ cup butter in a saucepan over low heat, add the flour, and cook until lightly browned, to make a roux. Add the roux to the pot, stirring well. Add the chopped chicken breast and Romano cheese and stir well. Add the cream, sherry, V-8 juice, and salt and heat for 10 minutes.

SERVES: 12

# Southwest Cream of Corn Soup with Serranos

This well-received classic is dramatically enhanced by floating large garlic croutons and a sprinkling of Parmesan cheese on top. It's great with any traditional Mexican or Southwestern fare, such as enchiladas or chiles rellenos.

1½ quarts water

2 tablespoons salt

6 ears fresh sweet corn, kernels cut off

8 serrano chiles, seeded, stemmed, and minced

1 large green bell pepper, seeded, stemmed, and finely chopped

1 large red bell pepper, seeded, stemmed, and finely chopped

2 medium red onions, finely chopped

½ cup red wine vinegar

½ cup dry red wine

3 ripe tomatoes, peeled, seeded, and finely chopped

½ bunch green onions, top 2 inches of green removed, cut into ¼-inch pieces

½ tablespoon minced garlic

1 tablespoon minced fresh parsley

2 tablespoons New Mexican red chile powder (Chimayo preferred)

1½ tablespoons sugar

½ cup shredded carrots

5 cups White Sauce #1 or #2 (pages 23-24)

Chopped fresh cilantro, for garnish

In a stockpot, combine the water, salt, corn, serranos, bell peppers, ½ of the red onion, ¼ cup of the vinegar, ¼ cup of the wine, tomatoes, green onions, garlic, parsley, and chile powder and bring to a boil. Boil uncovered for 10 minutes, stirring occasionally. Reduce the heat to low and simmer for 5 minutes.

In a bowl, combine the remaining red onion, remaining ¼ cup of the wine vinegar, and remaining ¼ cup of the red wine and let stand for 20 minutes.

In another bowl, combine the sugar, carrots, and white sauce. When the onions are finished marinating, transfer them and 2 tablespoons of the marinade to the white sauce.

Add the white sauce and onion mixture to the simmering stockpot. Blending with a whisk, cook for 5 minutes. Serve immediately or hold warm in the top of a double boiler. Garnish with the cilantro.

SERVES: 8 TO 10

# Conch Bisque

Conch is a dish of great pride wherever it is served—the acclaim comes from both the meat and the fine shell. A very popular dish in the Turks and Caicos, this conch bisque doesn't have the tomatoes that are so popular in Caribbean conch dishes. The flavor comes from heavily pounded conchs, good white wine, thyme, and hot peppers. Since the soup tends to be rather rich, we suggest serving it as a light lunch or dinner entrée. Squid may be substituted for the conch.

6 conchs, cleaned, pounded with a heavy mallet to flatten it,
   and diced into ½ inch pieces
5 cups water or Traditional European Fish Stock (page 18)
1 cup dry white wine, plus more to be used for cooking liquid
2 tablespoons butter plus 2 tablespoons vegetable oil (or use
   all vegetable oil)
1 cup chopped onions
1½ cups chopped green bell pepper
1 cup chopped celery
2 cloves garlic, minced
2 teaspoons fresh thyme or 1 teaspoon dried thyme
2 medium potatoes, peeled and diced into ½-inch cubes
1 cup diced carrots
1 large habanero chile, stemmed, seeded, and minced
3 tablespoons chives, chopped
1 cup half-and-half
Salt and pepper to taste

Place the pounded conch, 5 cups of water, and 1 cup of wine in a heavy stockpot and bring the mixture to a hard boil. Lower the heat so the liquid is at a light rolling boil and boil for 45 minutes. Remove the mixture from the heat and strain and measure the liquid; add more white wine to make 6 cups of liquid. Reserve the conch meat.

Wash the pot and pour the 6 cups of liquid back into the pot. Bring the liquid to a boil.

While the conch mixture is cooking, heat the oil and butter mixture in a heavy skillet and sauté the onions, bell pepper, celery, and the garlic over a low heat for 1 minute. Add the thyme and stir it into the sauté.

Add the sautéed mixture to the boiling conch liquid, and add the potatoes, carrots, habanero chile, chives, and the conch meat. Bring the mixture back to a boil, lower the heat, and simmer for 1 hour.

Remove the pot from the heat and let it cool slightly. Stir in the half-and-half, salt, and pepper and reheat the soup, taking care not to let it boil.

SERVES: 6 TO 8

# Colombian Coconut Soup

This recipe hails from the tropical lowlands of the Republic of Colombia, where it is known, logically, as *sopa de coco*. Coconuts are frequently used in cooking there. Tortillas cut into strips and fried in vegetable oil are a nice accompaniment. To really dress it up, serve in coconut shell halves.

2 large ripe coconuts, cracked, meat grated

2 cups milk, scalded

3 cups Traditional European Fish Stock (page 18) or
    Mountain Road Cafe Classic Chicken Stock (page 15)

2 egg yolks, well beaten

½ habanero chile, or 1 ½ jalapeños, seeded, stemmed, and
    minced

Paprika to taste

Salt to taste

Combine the grated coconut and the milk. Let cool, then squeeze through cheesecloth or a linen napkin to extract all liquid. Combine the coconut milk, stock, egg yolks, and chile in a stockpot and simmer for 10 minutes, stirring constantly. To serve, sprinkle with paprika and salt, and accompany with strips of crispy tortillas.

SERVES: 4

# Curried Coconut Soup

From South America to Africa, we now make a coconut culinary leap. The hot curry powder blends nicely with the cool coconut milk to create a tangy Nigerian soup. Curry has traveled around the world, and every country has its own variation on the spice blend. Here we call for a hot Indian curry powder in combination with freshly grated ginger.

3 cups coconut milk

3 cups Mountain Road Cafe Classic Chicken Stock (page 15)

2 teaspoons imported Indian curry powder

½ teaspoon salt

¼ teaspoon freshly ground white pepper

¼ cup prepared grated coconut

1 tablespoon freshly grated ginger

¼ teaspoon cornstarch

½ cup plain yogurt, for garnish

¼ cup toasted coconut, for garnish

Minced parsley, for garnish

Combine the coconut milk and 2¾ cups of the stock in a large, heavy stockpot and bring to a boil. Reduce the heat slightly. Add the curry powder, salt, pepper, coconut, and grated ginger, and simmer for 10 minutes.

Mix the cornstarch with the remaining ¼ cup stock and add it in a steady stream to the simmering soup, stirring constantly. Heat until the soup thickens slightly. Serve the soup hot with all of the garnishes.

SERVES: 4 TO 6

LEMONGRASS-GINGERED CHICKEN
WONTON SOUP (PAGE 117)

ACORN SQUASH AND CORN
STEW WITH CHIPOTLE (PAGE 81)

CREAMY GREEN CHILE AND
BAY SHRIMP CHOWDER (PAGE 34)

# Newspaper Soup

This highly unusual soup is not really a bisque or cream soup—it just resembles one. W.C. says that the soup is so named because it is black and white and red all over. It requires three processes to complete, which is a little more work than most soups in this book, but is well worth it. Note that the recipe requires advance preparation. It freezes well so you can amaze your friends and relatives time and time again.

Part 1:

3 quarts Mountain Road Cafe Classic Chicken Stock (page 15) or Vibrant Vegetable Stock (page 19)

2 cups Great Northern beans, soaked overnight

1 medium onion, minced

3 tablespoons minced garlic

1 medium leek, white part only, finely chopped

½ teaspoon ground bay leaf

1 tablespoon finely ground white pepper

2 tablespoons salt

½ teaspoon ground celery seed

2 tablespoons minced fresh parsley

½ teaspoon freshly ground nutmeg

2 tablespoons white sugar

3 tablespoons freshly squeezed lemon juice

Part 2:

3 quarts Basic Beef Stock (page 14) or Vibrant Vegetable Stock (page 19)

2 cups black beans, soaked overnight in water

1 medium onion, minced

5 tablespoons minced garlic

¾ teaspoon ground bay leaf

1½ tablespoons finely ground black pepper

2 tablespoons salt

½ teaspoon ground celery seed

1 teaspoon freshly ground cinnamon

1 tablespoon minced fresh oregano

2 tablespoons dark brown sugar

¼ cup freshly squeezed lime juice (Key lime preferred)

PART 3:

½ tablespoon garlic

4 tablespoons olive oil

¼ teaspoon fresh ground nutmeg

5 tablespoons mayonnaise

3 tablespoons sour cream

½ teaspoon salt (optional)

4 tablespoons hot red chile powder (Chimayo preferred)

¼ cup tomato paste

To make the black and white soups, use two large stockpots. For part 1, combine all ingredients except the sugar and lemon juice in one pot. For part 2, combine all ingredients except the brown sugar and lime juice in the other pot. Bring both pots to a boil and continue boiling, uncovered, until the beans are soft, about 1 hour. Add water if necessary.

While the soups are cooking, make part 3. Slightly spread the cloves apart in the heads of garlic and pour 1 tablespoon of olive oil over each head. Roast the heads on a cookie sheet in a 375° oven for 20 minutes. Remove, cool, and squeeze the soft pulp from the cloves. In a food processor, combine the garlic with the remaining 1 tablespoon of olive oil, nutmeg, mayonnaise, sour cream, salt, and chile powder, and process until smooth. Place the purée in a squeeze bottle.

Remove the soups from the heat and cool. Purée both soups separately in a food processor, adding the sugar and lemon juice to part 1 and the brown sugar and lime juice to part 2. Return the soups to their pots and heat, taking care not to boil.

To serve, use shallow soup bowls and simultaneously ladle the black and white soups into the bowls so that half of the bowl is black and the other half is white in a "yin-yang" effect. Then paint ¼-inch-thick red ribbons of the garlic and chile purée over the top. Be creative—this is the fun part!

SERVES: 8 TO 10

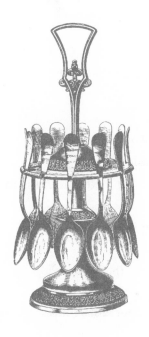

# Cream of Roma Tomato Soup
# with Jalapeños

This creamy pink soup is simply classic, and one of the best tomato soups we've ever tasted! Feel free to substitute habaneros for an even greater chile kick. This soup can precede any entrée, or accompany a sandwich for a light lunch.

2 cups White Sauce #1 or #2 (pages 23-24)
2 cups chopped Roma tomatoes
⅓ cup tomato paste
1 large onion, minced
¾ tablespoon minced garlic
¼ cup Chianti (or any dry red wine)
¾ tablespoon sugar
1 teaspoon salt
½ teaspoon finely ground white pepper
½ tablespoon balsamic vinegar
2 jalapeños, seeded, stemmed, and minced
⅔ cup heavy cream
1 tablespoon minced fresh basil

In a stockpot, combine the white sauce, tomatoes, tomato paste, onion, garlic, Chianti, sugar, salt, pepper, vinegar, and jalapeños. Simmer over low heat for 20 minutes. Do not boil. Blend in the cream and basil and gently warm.

SERVES: 4

# Creamy Green Chile Chicken Soup

HEAT SCALE: MEDIUM

Here's a Southwestern classic featuring New Mexican green chiles. It is one of the favorites at W.C.'s Mountain Road Cafe. If W.C. should forget to post it for a while on his specials board, his regulars complain loudly. Serve it before any Mexican or Southwestern entrées or grilled meats.

6 cups W.C.'s Green Chile Sauce (page 26)

2 cups White Sauce #2 (page 24)

1 cup Mountain Road Cafe Classic Chicken Stock (page 15)

1 (3½-pound) chicken, poached, skin and bones removed, and chopped

½ teaspoon salt

½ teaspoon finely ground white pepper

¼ teaspoon dried Mexican oregano

1 cup heavy cream

In a large stockpot, heat the Green Chile Sauce, White Sauce #2, and chicken stock, stirring well with a whisk. Add the remaining ingredients, stir well and simmer, uncovered, for 10 minutes.

SERVES: 8

# Sweet Potato Chipotle Chile Bisque

HEAT SCALE: HOT

This elegant soup is rich both in color and taste. The smoky accent of the chipotle chiles complements the sweetness of the potatoes. The silky texture of this soup encourages second helpings.

3 pounds sweet potatoes

1 tablespoon olive oil

4 large dried chipotle chiles

¼ cup dark rum

½ cup water

4 cups White Sauce #2 (page 24)

2 cups milk

⅔ cup Vibrant Vegetable Stock (page 19) or Mountain Road
    Cafe Classic Chicken Stock (page 15)

3 tablespoons sour cream

2 tablespoons dark brown sugar

1 tablespoon raw honey (the darker the better)

½ tablespoon molasses

1 teaspoon five-spice powder

½ teaspoon cinnamon

½ teaspoon salt

⅛ teaspoon vanilla

Lemon zest, for garnish

Wash the sweet potatoes well using a vegetable brush and soak in water for 5 minutes after cleaning. Dry and rub with olive oil. Puncture the sweet potatoes with a knife point about 5 times. Place the sweet potatoes in a shallow baking dish and bake at 375° for about 1¼ hours. Add a little water to the baking dish after 15 minutes to keep the potatoes from scorching. Test with a knife for softness, remove and set aside to cool. Scoop all the flesh out of the jackets and reserve.

While the sweet potatoes are baking, soak the chipotles in a bowl filled with the rum and water, using another bowl to keep them submerged. When they are soft after about 1 hour, purée the chipotles and the soaking mixture in a blender and reserve.

In a stockpot, heat the white sauce, gradually adding the milk and stock and stirring with a whisk. Add the remaining ingredients, except the zest, stir well, and simmer for 5 minutes. Add the reserved sweet potato, stir well, and simmer for 5 minutes. Just before serving, swirl in the reserved chipotle liquid. Serve garnished with the lemon zest.

SERVES: 8

# Cream of Poblano Chile Soup with Grilled Chicken

HEAT SCALE: MILD

Here's the ultimate creamed chile soup, which uses large amounts of the mild, flavorful poblano chiles, counterbalanced by the smoky flavor of the grilled chicken. This soup cries out for a cold glass of your favorite dry white wine.

4 tablespoons butter

1 pound poblano chiles, seeded, stemmed, and chopped

½ medium onion, chopped

¼ teaspoon minced garlic

1 medium red bell pepper, seeded, stemmed, and chopped

¼ teaspoon ground marjoram

¼ teaspoon dried thyme

¼ teaspoon dried basil

3 tablespoons white wine

3 cups White Sauce #1 or #2 (pages 23–24)

½ cup heavy cream

½ cup Mountain Road Cafe Classic Chicken Stock (page 15)

¼ cup teriyaki sauce

¾ teaspoon sugar

⅛ teaspoon vanilla

¾ teaspoon salt

1 teaspoon minced parsley

Pinch fresh nutmeg

1 pound boneless chicken breasts, grilled and finely chopped

Melt the butter in a skillet and sauté the chiles, onion, garlic, bell pepper, marjoram, thyme, and basil for 5 minutes, slowly adding the wine. Remove from the heat, place in a food processor or blender, and purée. Reserve.

Over low heat, in a stockpot, warm the White Sauce. With a whisk, stir in the cream and chicken stock and mix well. Add the teriyaki, sugar, vanilla, salt, parsley, nutmeg, and chicken. Hold at a low simmer, taking care not to boil the mixture. Add the chile purée mixture and simmer, uncovered, for 5 minutes before serving.

SERVES: 6

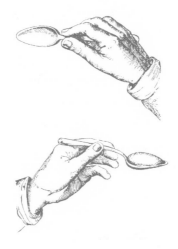

# 4.
# Searing Seafood Soups and Chowders

## Key West Conch Chowder

🔥 🔥 🔥                    HEAT SCALE: HOT

Here's a key soup from W.C.'s establishment in Key West, the Portside Restaurant. Conch is so revered in Key West that the locals call themselves "Conchs." Naturally, every cook on the island has their own "best and true" conch chowder. But take our word—this one is the best of them all. Serve with an ice cold beer and hunk of Cuban bread, and finish with Key lime pie for dessert.

2 tablespoons vegetable oil

½ pound smoked bacon, cut crosswise into strips

3 pounds coarsely ground conch meat

4 medium green bell peppers, chopped

4 jalapeños, seeded, stemmed, and minced

4 large celery stalks, finely chopped

2 medium onions, finely chopped

4 cups water

6 medium potatoes, peeled and diced

1 quart peeled, seeded, and crushed Roma tomatoes

⅔ cup tomato purée

1 cup tomato juice

1½ tablespoons minced garlic

¾ tablespoon cayenne

¾ tablespoon finely ground white pepper

4 bay leaves

In a skillet, heat the vegetable oil and bacon and cook over medium heat until the bacon is crisp. Remove with a slotted spoon and drain on paper towels.

Add the conch, bell pepper, jalapeños, celery, and onions to the skillet and sauté for 5 minutes, stirring well. Turn off the heat, transfer the mixture to a stockpot, and add the water a cup at a time, stirring well. Add the remaining ingredients, bring to a boil, and boil until the potatoes are soft, about 15 minutes.

SERVES: 8 TO 10

# Striped Bass Bouillabaisse with Rouille

The French have so many contradictory rules and regulations regarding this dish that we have taken some liberties, such as substituting striped bass for the traditional scorpion fish. Many recipes include shellfish and lobster, but we have opted just for the black mussels. Feel free to add scallops or other seafood to this soup. We've been known to cook this one up right after our striped bass fishing trips on Elephant Butte Lake in southern New Mexico!

FOR THE BOUILLON:

¾ cup olive oil

2 cups thinly sliced onions

1 cup thinly sliced leeks

4 cups water

2 cups dry white wine

2 pounds fish heads, bones, and trimmings

3 pounds ripe tomatoes, coarsely chopped

½ teaspoon dried fennel seed, crushed

2 cloves garlic, minced

1 (3-inch) piece orange peel

1 teaspoon dried thyme

2 sprigs parsley

1 bay leaf

¼ teaspoon crushed saffron threads

Salt to taste

Finely ground black pepper to taste

4 pounds striped bass (or other firm white fish), cut into
   2-inch cubes

2 pounds live black mussels or clams

2 cups Rouille (page 10)

Heat the oil in a heavy, 4- to 6-quart stockpot and add the onions and leeks. Cook over medium heat until they are tender, but not brown. Add the water, wine, fish trimmings, tomatoes, herbs, and seasonings, and cook, uncovered, over medium heat for 30 minutes.

When the bouillon is done, strain the mixture through a fine sieve into a soup pot, pressing the fish trimmings and vegetables to squeeze out all the juices. Bring the strained stock to a boil and add the fish. Cook for 5 minutes, then add the mussels or clams and cook for 5 minutes.

Serve the soup with the Rouille and pieces of French bread.

SERVES: 6 TO 8

# Veracruz-Style Shrimp Chowder

Dried shrimp and epazote are available in Latin and Asian markets, and really intensify the flavor of this dish. Unfortunately, there is no substitute for epazote, with its unique, pungent flavor. Serve over cooked rice and garnish with lemon.

8 cloves garlic, unpeeled

2 chipotle chiles, seeded and stemmed

2 ancho chiles, seeded and stemmed

1 onion, cut into eighths

3 tomatoes, peeled and cut into quarters

3 tablespoons oil

3 cups water or Traditional European Fish Stock (page 18)

8 dried shrimp

¼ cup dried and crumbled epazote

2 pounds fresh shrimp, shelled

Wrap the cloves of garlic in aluminum foil and roast them in a 400° oven for 30 minutes. When they are cool enough to handle, squeeze the garlic out of its skin into a blender.

Using a dry skillet, lightly roast the chiles for 2 minutes, taking care not to burn them. Add the chiles to the blender along with the onion and the tomatoes and purée the mixture.

Heat the oil in a medium skillet, pour in the puréed mixture, and cook it over a medium-low heat for 1 minute. Add the water, dried shrimp, and the epazote and simmer for 3 minutes.

Add the fresh shrimp and simmer the mixture for an additional 5 minutes, or until the shrimp are cooked. Add more water if the mixture starts to get too thick. Serve immediately.

SERVES: 4

# Rock Shrimp Gumbo with Tabasco and Cayenne

Be sure to buy these shrimp with their rock-hard shell already removed. Rock shrimp have more flavor than other shrimp, but removing the shells is extremely difficult—hence the name. Serve this over some "dirty rice" with a side of cornbread for a Louisiana treat.

¼ cup olive oil

1½ pounds okra, stems removed, thinly sliced

½ cup (4 ounces) butter

1 large green bell pepper, seeded and chopped

1½ medium onions, chopped

2 tablespoons minced garlic

2 tablespoons flour

4 cups Mountain Road Cafe Classic Chicken Stock (page 15)

3 medium tomatoes, peeled and chopped

½ teaspoon white pepper

½ teaspoon dried thyme

1 teaspoon salt

2 tablespoons tomato paste

2 pounds rock shrimp, peeled

¾ pound crabmeat

1 tablespoon Tabasco sauce

1½ tablespoons Worcestershire sauce

½ teaspoon cayenne

Heat the olive oil in a skillet and add the okra. Cook, stirring constantly, for 5 minutes. Set aside.

In a stockpot, heat the butter and add the bell pepper, onions, and garlic and cook until the onions are soft, about 4 minutes. Add the flour and stir until it is well mixed. Add the stock, stirring briskly with a whisk until well blended. Add the reserved okra, tomatoes, pepper, thyme, salt, tomato paste, rock shrimp, and crabmeat and simmer over low heat, covered, for 20 minutes. Add the remaining ingredients, stir well, cook for 10 more minutes, and serve.

SERVES: 6 TO 8

# Poor Man's Lobster Gumbo

            HEAT SCALE: MEDIUM

Monkfish is called "poor man's lobster" because its flavor is similar to lobster but its price tag isn't. It is a firm fish that does well in a delicious gumbo such as this, and the payoff is in the praise you'll receive. When making the roux, heat the shortening until it smokes a bit, and the resulting roux will be perfectly browned.

7 tablespoons vegetable shortening

1 pound okra, cut into ½-inch rounds

2 cups chopped tomatoes

2 tablespoons tomato paste

¼ cup flour

3 medium onions, chopped

3 stalks celery, cut into ½-inch pieces

1½ tablespoons minced garlic

1 medium red bell pepper, diced

1 medium green bell pepper, diced

4 cups Mountain Road Cafe Chicken Stock (page 15)

2 cups Traditional European Fish Stock (page 18)

2½ pounds monkfish, cut into 1-inch cubes
1½ tablespoons cayenne
1½ tablespoons Tabasco sauce
Salt to taste

In a stockpot, melt 4 tablespoons of the shortening over medium heat and add the okra, tomatoes, and tomato paste. Cook, stirring occasionally, for 15 minutes.

In another stockpot, melt the remaining 3 tablespoons of shortening, add the flour, and heat, stirring well, until a roux is formed. Add the onions, celery, garlic, and bell peppers, and remove from the heat for 5 minutes. Add this mixture to the tomato mixture, stir well, and add the remaining ingredients.

Cook, uncovered, over medium heat for 20 minutes, stirring occasionally and adding water if the gumbo is too thick.

SERVES: 8 TO 10

# Basque-Style Bonito Tomato Chowder

W.C. recommends using bonito (a dark-fleshed type of fish that is related to tuna) in this hearty chowder, but any variety of tuna will work. Some people object to strongly flavored fish like the bonito, but we love it. The Spanish brandy and tomatoes give this chowder a distinctly Basque edge. Serve this with a hard, crusty bread.

2 medium onions, chopped

½ cup extra virgin olive oil

6 medium very ripe tomatoes, peeled, seeded, and finely chopped

1 teaspoon dried thyme

2 tablespoons minced fresh parsley

1 tablespoon Spanish brandy or cognac

3 dried red New Mexican chile pods, seeded and stemmed

2 tablespoons minced garlic

1 tablespoon freshly ground black pepper

1 tablespoon salt

2 medium green bell peppers, finely chopped

¾ pound Red Bliss potatoes, peeled and cut into ½-inch cubes

3 cups hot water or Traditional European Fish Stock (page 18)

1½ pounds fresh bonito or tuna, cut into 1-inch cubes

In a stockpot, combine 2 tablespoons of the chopped onion with 2 tablespoons of the olive oil and sauté until the onion is translucent, about 3 minutes. Add the tomatoes, thyme, parsley, brandy, chile pods, garlic, pepper, and salt. Cover the pot and cook over medium heat for 20 minutes.

Remove from the heat and allow to cool. Place the tomato mixture in batches in a food processor or blender and purée until smooth.

In another pot, combine the remaining onion and the remaining olive oil, and sauté over medium heat for about 7 minutes. Add the bell pepper and potatoes and cook for 2 minutes, stirring often. Add the hot water and bring to a boil for 20 minutes. Add the reserved tomato purée and the bonito or tuna, and lower the heat. Cover and simmer until the fish is flaky, about 10 to 12 minutes. Serve as quickly as possible from the pot.

SERVES: 6 TO 8

# Callaloo and Crab Soup

HEAT SCALE: MEDIUM

Dave created this recipe after collecting it from friends in Trinidad (where he ate this soup at every opportunity in order to sample its multiple variations). This particular recipe is a favorite variation featuring crabmeat, a common and tasty addition to this bright green soup. Callaloo, also called dasheen, is the top leaves of the taro plant. Spinach can successfully substitute for the hard-to-find callaloo. This soup is considered to be one of the national dishes of Trinidad and Tobago.

2 tablespoons butter, plus 1 tablespoon, for optional garnish
1 medium onion, diced
½ cup chopped celery
1 clove garlic, minced
1 quart Mountain Road Cafe Classic Chicken Stock (page 15)
1 cup coconut milk

½ pound diced smoked ham, or 1 small ham hock

2½ cups washed, coarsely chopped, firmly packed callaloo or
    spinach leaves

1 cup sliced okra

1 teaspoon dried thyme

¼ teaspoon freshly ground black pepper

1 Congo pepper or habanero, seeded, stemmed, and minced

1 pound cooked crabmeat, chopped

Salt to taste

Heat 2 tablespoons of the butter in a large stockpot and sauté the onion, celery, and garlic for 2 to 3 minutes. Add the chicken stock, coconut milk, and ham and bring to a boil. Add the callaloo or spinach, the okra, thyme, black pepper, and the Congo or habanero pepper.

Reduce the heat to a simmer and cook, covered, for about 50 minutes, stirring occasionally, until the callaloo is thoroughly cooked.

Whisk the soup until very smooth, or purée it in small batches in a blender. Add the crabmeat and heat thoroughly. Melt the 1 tablespoon of butter for garnish and drizzle it over the top. Add salt to taste.

SERVES: 8 TO 10

# Chilled Bloody Mary Soup with Clams

HEAT SCALE: MEDIUM  🔥 🔥

W.C. heard the story that this soup was designed as a plot to evade New York's Sunday liquor laws. Then he visited the Mystic Yacht Club, where he was introduced to the concept of raw clam Bloody Marys. So he cheerfully stole both ideas and came up with this soup. In his version, the clams are slightly cooked by the hot soup before it is chilled.

1 medium onion, finely chopped

4 stalks celery, diced

2 tablespoons butter

2 tablespoons tomato paste

1½ tablespoons sugar

5 cups V-8 Juice

2 tablespoons Worcestershire sauce

1 teaspoon Tabasco sauce

1 teaspoon salt

½ teaspoon cayenne

1½ tablespoons lemon juice

6 fresh cherrystone clams, minced

¾ cup pepper-flavored vodka

Cucumber spears, for garnish

In a stockpot, sauté the onion and celery in the butter for 2 minutes. Add the tomato paste and sugar, stir well, and cook for 1 minute. Add the V-8 Juice, Worcestershire, Tabasco, salt, and cayenne and bring to a boil. Turn off the heat, stir in the remaining ingredients, and chill until very cold. Serve garnished with the cucumber spears.

SERVES: 2

# Roasted Pepper and Mussel Soup

This recipe is another example of highly unlikely combinations that really work together in a soup—this time beets, peppers, and mussels. It has great color, great flavor, and trace minerals you didn't even know you were missing!

2 medium beets, peeled

2 quarts water

1 pound green lip mussels from New Zealand, scrubbed

½ cup plus 3 tablespoons olive oil

¼ cup dry sherry

10 fresh New Mexican chiles, red preferred

2 tablespoons butter

1 head garlic, roasted, peeled, and coarsely chopped

2 small carrots, peeled and thinly sliced

2 shallots, minced

2 cups Mountain Road Cafe Classic Chicken Stock (page 15)
    or Vibrant Vegetable Stock (page 19)

1 teaspoon red wine vinegar

½ teaspoon white wine vinegar

¼ teaspoon cayenne

2 jalapeños, seeded, stemmed, and minced

½ teaspoon salt

¼ teaspoon freshly ground black pepper

In a stockpot, combine the beets and the water. Boil for 40 minutes, then remove the beets, cool, and thinly slice. Reserve.

To prepare the mussels, remove ½ of the shell of each one by cutting into the hinge and twisting, with a table knife, along the rim.

Discard the top shell and brush the mussels with 1 tablespoon of the olive oil. Place the mussels, open side down, on a grill (or up under a broiler) and cook for 2 minutes. Remove from the grill, sprinkle liberally with the sherry, return to the grill, and cook for 2 more minutes. Remove from the grill, cool, and cut the mussels into fourths. Reserve the meat and discard the shells.

Place the chiles on a grill or under the broiler, and heat until they blister and slightly blacken. Place the chiles in a covered container just large enough to accommodate them (or wrap in foil) and let stand for 10 minutes. Remove the skin, stems, and seeds. Place the chiles in a food processor or blender with the ½ cup olive oil and purée. Set the purée aside.

Heat the remaining 2 tablespoons of olive oil and the butter in a stockpot over medium heat, and add the reserved beets, garlic, carrots, and shallots. Cook for 7 minutes, stirring occasionally. Do not brown them. Add the remaining ingredients, stir well, and remove from the heat. Cool and purée in a food processor or blender.

Return the soup to the pot, add the mussels and puréed chiles, and cook over low heat for about 15 minutes. Serve immediately.

SERVES: 4

# Sweet and Spicy Lobster Tail Soup

🔥 🔥 🔥                    HEAT SCALE: HOT

This unusual seafood soup with an Asian flair owes its unique flavor to marinating the lobster tails for at least an hour before proceeding to make the soup. Note that this recipe requires some advance preparation.

3 pounds lobster tails in the shell, about 6

2 cups teriyaki sauce

2 cups rice vinegar

1 tablespoon freshly grated, peeled ginger

3½ tablespoons minced garlic

3½ teaspoons five-spice powder

1 tablespoon brown sugar

½ cup rice wine or any dry white wine

1 cup green gunpowder tea

6 cups Mountain Road Cafe Classic Chicken Stock (page 15)

1 cup Traditional European Fish Stock (page 18)

12 Thai chiles, seeded, stemmed, and minced, or 6 serranos
    or jalapeños

¼ cup soy sauce

2 tablespoons freshly squeezed lemon juice

¼ cup honey

½ tablespoon ground ginger

In a bowl, combine the lobster tails with the teriyaki sauce, rice vinegar, grated ginger, 1½ tablespoons of the garlic, 1½ teaspoons of the five-spice powder, and the brown sugar and marinate for at least 1 hour. Remove the lobster tails and discard the marinade.

In a wok, heat the wine and tea and add the lobster tails. Cover and cook 5 to 10 minutes. Remove the lobster tails and let cool. Remove the meat from the shells, coarsely chop it, and reserve. Discard the shells and the liquid.

In a stockpot, combine the chicken stock, fish stock, chiles, soy sauce, lemon juice, honey, the remaining 2 tablespoons of the garlic, ground ginger, and the remaining 2 teaspoons of the five-spice powder and boil for 15 minutes. Add the lobster meat, turn off the heat and allow to sit for 5 minutes, then serve.

SERVES: 6

# W.C.'s Double Clam
# Rio Grande Chowder

🔥 🔥          HEAT SCALE: MEDIUM

Clams along the Rio Grande? Anything's possible in these days of twenty-four-hour deliveries of fresh seafood, even in the desert. The combination of clams and green chile is unbeatable.

1½ cups Traditional European Fish Stock (page 18)

3 cups chopped clams

5 cups White Sauce #1 or #2 (pages 23-24)

½ teaspoon ground ginger

1 tablespoon minced garlic

1 tablespoon minced fresh parsley

1½ teaspoons Old Bay seasoning

½ cup tomato juice

2 cups W.C.'s Green Chile Sauce (page 26)

1 tablespoon vegetable oil

1 medium onion, minced

2 cups diced, peeled potatoes

¾ cup diced, peeled carrots

¼ cup white wine

2 tablespoons sugar

1 tablespoon Tabasco sauce

1 teaspoon Worcestershire Sauce

1 cup half-and-half

In a large stockpot, combine the fish stock and the clams and bring to a boil. Reduce the heat to medium and whisk in the white sauce.

Then add the ginger, garlic, parsley, Old Bay seasoning, tomato juice, and green chile sauce. Stir well, lower the heat to very low, and simmer, uncovered, for 15 minutes, stirring occasionally.

Meanwhile, heat the oil in another pan, add the onion, potatoes, and carrots and sauté for 5 minutes, stirring well. Add the wine in small quantities over the next 10 minutes, stirring well. Add the remaining ingredients and stir well. Add this onion and potato mixture to the simmering clam mixture and serve hot.

SERVES: 8 TO 10

# Chilled Cucumber and
# Bay Shrimp Soup

HEAT SCALE: MILD TO HOT,
DEPENDING ON THE VARIETY OF CHILE

Here's another unusual flavor combination that makes a great cold soup. W.C. prefers to use datil peppers from St. Augustine in this soup, but unless you're growing them yourself, they can be hard to find, so we've listed some alternatives.

1 tablespoon minced datil, bell, or habanero pepper

3 cups Mountain Road Cafe Classic Chicken Stock (page 15)
   or Vibrant Vegetable Stock (page 19)

6 cucumbers, peeled, seeded, and chopped

1 cup plain yogurt

⅓ cup freshly squeezed lemon juice

¾ cup bay shrimp

1 tablespoon butter

1 teaspoon white pepper

3 cups chilled heavy cream

Salt to taste

1 bunch fresh dill, for garnish

In a food processor, combine the pepper, chicken stock, cucumbers, yogurt, and lemon juice and purée until smooth.

In a heavy skillet, sauté the shrimp in the butter and white pepper for 2 minutes. Set aside and let cool. In a bowl, combine the purée, the shrimp, and the cream and chill in the refrigerator for 2 hours. Adjust the salt, and serve garnished with sprigs of dill.

SERVES: 6

# Snapper, Chicken and Wild Rose Chowder

HEAT SCALE: MILD

Here's a soup almost impossible to classify: it contains snapper, but also chicken and rice. The flavors of the raisinlike pasilla chiles and the marinated rose petals add more dimensions to this unusual soup.

3 whole pasilla chiles, seeded and stemmed
10 cups Mountain Road Cafe Classic Chicken Stock (page 15)
1½ pounds red snapper fillets, cut into ¼-inch cubes
1 cup cooked long-grain rice
¾ pound boned and skinned chicken breast, diced
1 tablespoon minced fresh parsley
8 fresh wild or Rambling Rose blossoms, saving only the
   petals
6 limes, cut in half
3 tablespoons sugar
1 tablespoon hearty red wine
1 teaspoon Mexican vanilla

In a large stockpot, combine the chiles and the chicken stock and boil. Reduce the stock to two-thirds of its original volume, strain, and discard the chiles. Add the snapper, rice, chicken, and parsley, reduce the heat, and simmer, uncovered, for 10 minutes.

Place the rose petals in a medium-sized bowl and squeeze the limes over them evenly. In a small bowl, combine the sugar, wine, and vanilla, stir well, and drizzle over the petals. Marinate the petals for 15 minutes, and serve in warm bowls with the petals spooned over the top.

SERVES: 6 TO 8

# 5.
# Volcanic Vegetarian Soups

## White and Blue Tortilla Chili

HEAT SCALE: MEDIUM

This is a highly unusual version of chili that W.C. invented to use up an excess of tortillas. This is an example of a happy accident in a well-stocked kitchen, and good cooks tend to have a lot of those, so feel free to experiment.

2 cups peeled, seeded, and puréed tomatoes

2 medium onions, minced

6 large cloves garlic, minced

6 cups Vibrant Vegetable Stock (page 19)

1½ cups W.C.'s Chimayo Red Chile Sauce (page 29)

3 serrano or jalapeño chiles, seeded, stemmed, and minced

½ teaspoon salt

½ teaspoon sugar

Pinch ground cumin

2½ tablespoons vegetable shortening

8 white corn tortillas, cut into strips ¼ inch by 2 inches

8 blue corn tortillas, cut into strips ¼ inch by 2 inches

1 pound Monterey jack cheese, grated

3 tablespoons minced cilantro

In a stockpot, combine the tomatoes, onions, garlic, stock, W.C.'s Chimayo Red Chile Sauce, the serrano or jalapeño chiles, salt, sugar, and cumin and bring to a boil. Reduce the heat and simmer, uncovered, for 15 minutes.

In a heavy skillet, heat the shortening to medium hot and fry the tortilla strips until they are crisp, turning them constantly. Drain on paper towels.

Place the strips on the bottom of 8 soup bowls, reserving some of each color for garnish. Divide the cheese among the bowls. Add soup to each bowl, float the remaining tortilla strips on top, and garnish with the cilantro.

SERVES: 8

# Black Bean Chipotle Purée

This exciting, thick soup marries the dark colors and flavors of the beans with the chipotle chiles, but there's quite a few other flavorful ingredients as well. Serve this with a hearty bread and your favorite sharp cheese. Note that this recipe requires advance preparation.

2 quarts water
1 tablespoon salt
3 cups black beans, cleaned and soaked overnight
½ stalk celery, with leaves, chopped
3 cups dry red wine
3 large dried chipotle chiles, about 3 inches long
1 teaspoon freshly ground nutmeg
1 teaspoon freshly ground cinnamon
½ teaspoon ground ginger
1 tablespoon finely ground white pepper
2 tablespoons Mexican leaf oregano
½ cup chopped fresh parsley
1 tablespoon Worcestershire sauce
1 onion, coarsely chopped
3 tablespoons chopped garlic
1 cup chopped white button mushrooms
¼ cup extra virgin olive oil
¼ cup peanut oil
⅓ cup tomato purée
2½ tablespoons red wine vinegar

¾ cup raw honey

Lime wedges for garnish

Coarsely chopped cilantro, for garnish

In a large stockpot, combine the water, salt, black beans, celery, wine, chipotles, nutmeg, cinnamon, ginger, pepper, oregano, parsley, and Worcestershire sauce and bring to a boil.

In a skillet, combine the onion, garlic, mushrooms, olive oil, and peanut oil and sauté until the onion is soft. Add this mixture to the beans and boil until the beans are soft, about 2 hours (this can vary greatly, so check them as they're cooking). Add water as needed, but by the end there should be little water in the pot.

Allow the beans to cool. In a bowl, combine the tomato purée, vinegar, and honey and mix with the beans. Purée the beans in a food processor.

Reheat over very low heat (or use a double boiler), adding water to the desired consistency. Serve garnished with the lime wedges and chopped cilantro.

SERVES: 8 TO 10

# Wild Mushroom and Vegetable Gumbo with Jalapeños

🔥 🔥       HEAT SCALE: MEDIUM

This gumbo is unusual because it is vegetarian. Take your choice of three separate garnishes for this gumbo.

4 tablespoons vegetable shortening
4 tablespoons flour
4 cups Vibrant Vegetable Stock (page 19)
2 tablespoons butter
½ pound morels, chopped
½ pound chanterelles, chopped
1 medium onion, chopped
3 ears of corn, kernels cut off the cob
3 medium yellow tomatoes, chopped
3 medium red tomatoes, chopped
1 cup freshly shelled peas
1 medium red bell pepper, chopped
1 medium green bell pepper, chopped
2 jalapeños, seeded, stemmed, and minced
1 tablespoon minced garlic
Salsa, strips of lemon rind, or caramelized red onions, for
   garnish

In a stockpot, melt the shortening and whisk in the flour. Add the vegetable stock, whisk well, and hold at barely a simmer, uncovered.

In another stockpot, melt the butter and sauté the mushrooms and onion for 3 minutes. Add the remaining ingredients, except the garnishes, and cook over low heat, uncovered, for 10 minutes, stirring only to avoid sticking. Add the hot vegetable stock and cook,

**76** Volcanic Vegetarian Soups

covered, over low heat for 20 minutes, stirring occasionally. If the gumbo is too thick, add some water. Garnish with your favorite salsa, strips of lemon rind, or some caramelized red onions.

SERVES: 8 TO 10

# Cream of Turnip Soup with Garlic and Habanero

HEAT SCALE: HOT

We know what you're thinking: turnips? Well, when prepared in a spiced-up soup like this one, they are transformed. Both of us humbly admit that we love the turnip family, and that they add a great dimension to soups and stews. This soup stores well in the refrigerator but doesn't freeze well. Mixed herb croutons make a nice garnish.

2 quarts water

2 pounds turnips, peeled and diced

3 tablespoons butter

2 tablespoons finely chopped garlic

1½ teaspoons salt

3 cups Vibrant Vegetable Stock (page 19)

2 cups White Sauce #1 or #2 (pages 23-24)

1 cup heavy cream

1 habanero chile, seeded, stemmed, and minced

¼ cup chopped arugula

1 tablespoon sugar

1 teaspoon fresh lemon juice

Chopped parsley, for garnish

In a stockpot, combine the water, turnips, butter, garlic, and salt and boil until the turnips are soft, about 30 minutes, adding water if needed. Drain and return the turnips to the pot.

Combine the stock, white sauce, and heavy cream and add it to the turnips. Cook over low heat, stirring constantly.

Combine the habanero, arugula, sugar, and lemon juice and add it to the soup, stirring well. Garnish with parsley and serve.

SERVES: 6 TO 8

# Double Chile Vegetarian Stew

 HEAT SCALE: MEDIUM

Poblano chiles are used for their flavor and serrano chiles for their serious bite, in this hearty stew that's perfect for a crisp fall day. This is an understated fusion dish with vegetables from all over the globe. Serve this with sticks of cornbread.

2 pounds russet potatoes, peeled and chopped

2 large carrots, chopped

3 poblano chiles, roasted, peeled, seeded, stemmed, and chopped

1 bunch bok choy, chopped

1 bunch green onions, chopped

1 leek, white part only, cut into ¼-inch rings

1 large head cabbage, chopped

2 tablespoons red wine vinegar

2 tablespoons teriyaki sauce

¼ cup dry white wine

4 cups peeled, seeded, and chopped tomatoes

1 (12-ounce) can tomato purée

1 medium onion, finely chopped

6 serrano chiles, seeded, stemmed, and finely chopped

1 red bell pepper, seeded and finely chopped

3 cups Vibrant Vegetable Stock (page 19)

⅛ teaspoon freshly ground nutmeg

1 tablespoon salt

1¾ tablespoons sugar

1 teaspoon finely ground black pepper

Combine all ingredients in a stockpot and boil, uncovered, for 30 minutes.

SERVES: 6 TO 8

# Quick Southwestern Vegetarian Goulash

People constantly tell us that it's such a pain to cook beans that they would rather just buy them canned. We won't tell, but you'll pay more money for an inferior product. Once the beans are cooked, however, this is an incredibly quick soup to make. Serve with sour cream on the side, if you wish.

1 tablespoon extra virgin olive oil

1 cup chopped onion

¾ cup chopped bell pepper

1 tablespoon minced jalapeño chile

2 tablespoons minced garlic

3 cups tomato sauce

½ cup Chianti or any red wine

6 Roma tomatoes, peeled and chopped

2 cups cooked long-grain brown rice

2 cups Vibrant Vegetable Stock (page 19)

4 cups cooked black-eyed peas

4 cups cooked kidney beans

2 cups cooked pinto beans

1½ teaspoons salt

1 teaspoon ground oregano

½ teaspoon ground cumin

½ teaspoon ground bay leaf

2 tablespoons fresh chopped parsley

¼ cup teriyaki sauce

In a stockpot, combine the oil, onion, bell pepper, jalapeño, garlic, and tomato sauce and bring to a simmer. Add the Chianti, tomatoes, and rice and cook for 5 minutes. Add the remaining ingredients and simmer for 15 minutes. Adjust the water if necessary.

SERVES: 12

# Acorn Squash and Corn Stew with Chipotle

HEAT SCALE: MILD

There's a lot of rich, smoky flavors here for such a simple recipe. The chipotle used can be either rehydrated dried pods, which are then finely chopped, or the canned chipotles in adobo sauce. To prepare the acorn squash, cut them in half, remove the seeds, add 1 teaspoon butter to each half, and bake the squash at 350° for 1¼ hours.

1 tablespoon peanut oil

1 medium onion, chopped

1 tablespoon minced garlic

4 cups tomato sauce

2 tablespoons finely chopped chipotle chiles, rehydrated or canned

1 tablespoon salt

2 cups corn kernels cut from cobs

3 cups baked, soft acorn squash (about 2 medium squashes)

½ cup teriyaki sauce

3 cups water

3 cups Vibrant Vegetable Stock (page 19)

1 teaspoon ground cinnamon

½ teaspoon bay leaf

½ teaspoon vanilla

1 cup freshly squeezed orange juice

1 tablespoon sugar

1 tablespoon raw honey

1½ tablespoons freshly squeezed lime juice

Garlic croutons (page 22), for garnish

Heat the oil in a stockpot and add the onion and garlic. Sauté until the onion is soft, about 5 minutes. Add the tomato sauce, chiles, salt, and corn and cook, uncovered, over medium heat for 15 minutes.

Add the squash, teriyaki sauce, water, stock, cinnamon, bay leaf, and vanilla and cook, uncovered, for 20 minutes.

Combine the orange juice, sugar, honey, and lime juice in a bowl and add it to the stew. Heat for 5 minutes.

Serve sprinkled with garlic croutons.

SERVES: 8

# Rice, Beans, and Greens Stew
# with Cayenne

Here's one of our favorite stews that we transplanted from Valencia, Spain, and then fired up. It has a lot of W.C.'s favorite soup ingredients, especially the beans, greens, and turnips. We suggest serving this stew with corn bread or pan-fried corn cakes.

¾ pound dried white beans

3 quarts water

1 pound well-trimmed collard greens, chopped

1 teaspoon Hungarian hot paprika

2 onions, finely chopped

2 tablespoons finely chopped fresh parsley

⅛ teaspoon saffron

2 medium turnips, peeled and thinly sliced

2 quarts Vibrant Vegetable Stock (page 19)

1 tablespoon salt

½ teaspoon white pepper

2 teaspoons cayenne powder

1½ cups short-grain rice

Combine the beans and the water in a large stockpot and bring to a boil. Reduce the heat and cook, uncovered, for 1 hour. Drain the beans and return them to the pot. Add the remaining ingredients except the rice and cook, uncovered, for 30 minutes. Add the rice and cook, covered, for 25 minutes. Adjust the consistency of the stew with water, if needed.

SERVES: 8 TO 10

# Peanut-Piquín Soup

Each African state seems to have its own version of peanut or groundnut soup. It is pretty common all over the continent, but especially popular in western Africa. This soup can be made a day ahead to blend the flavors, and then carefully reheated. Serve with some chopped dried tropical fruits or a mango chutney for a nice variation.

1 pound shelled, roasted peanuts
1 tablespoon peanut oil
1 cup chopped onion
½ cup chopped carrots
3 dried, crushed piquín chiles, or 3 fresh jalapeños, seeded, stemmed, and minced
8 cups Vibrant Vegetable Stock (page 19)
¾ cup milk
1 tablespoon cornstarch
¾ cup cream
½ teaspoon salt
Chopped parsley, for garnish
Chopped chives, for garnish

Rub the skins off of the peanuts. Place them in a food processor and grind them to a very fine meal. Set aside. Heat the oil in a large stockpot and sauté the onion and carrots for 2 minutes. Add the chiles, the reserved nuts, and the stock and bring the mixture to a boil. Lower the heat to a simmer, and simmer uncovered for 1 hour, stirring occasionally.

Pour ½ cup of the milk into a small jar, add the cornstarch, and shake vigorously. Pour the mixture through a fine sieve into the soup and stir continuously for 1 minute. Add the remaining milk, cream, and salt. Simmer uncovered for 3 minutes. Do not allow the mixture to boil. Cover the soup and let it simmer for 30 minutes. Serve the soup hot, garnished with the parsley and chives.

SERVES: 6

# Curried Portobello Avocado Soup

HEAT SCALE: MILD

Was W.C. hallucinating when he dreamed up this flavor combination? If he wasn't when he started, he was after he enjoyed a bowl! It's truly a palate shocker and a wonderful soup.

3 tablespoons sweet butter
1 tablespoon minced garlic
4 cups finely sliced portobello mushroom caps
3 tablespoons dry white wine
1 cup chopped ripe avocado (Haas preferred)
1½ cups Vibrant Vegetable Stock (page 19)
1 cup White Sauce #1 or #2 (pages 23-24)
1 tablespoon hot curry powder (freshly ground or imported preferred)
1½ cups milk
½ cup heavy cream
Watercress, for garnish
¼ teaspoon dry sherry or lime juice (optional)

Heat the butter in a stockpot and add the garlic and portobellos. Sauté for 2 minutes, stirring well, then add the wine and sauté for another 2 minutes, or until the portobellos are soft and dark.

Purée the remaining ingredients in a blender or food processor and add to the pot. Cook over medium heat, stirring well, but do not boil.

Garnish with the watercress. If desired, drizzle the sherry or lime juice on top of each bowl of soup just prior to serving.

SERVES: 6

# Chipotle Tomato Soup con Queso

        HEAT SCALE: MEDIUM

Here's a different twist on two standards, tomato soup and chile con queso, usually more of a dip than a soup. If chipotle powder is not available, use 2 teaspoons of canned chipotle in adobo, minced. Use a high-quality Swiss cheese for a high-quality taste.

¼ cup olive oil

3 medium onions, finely chopped

2 tablespoons minced garlic

1 cup minced mushrooms of your choice

1 tablespoon minced fresh parsley

2 cups minced celery with leaves

8 cups fresh Roma tomatoes, peeled, seeded, and puréed

1 cup tomato paste

2 cups tomato sauce

3 cups Vibrant Vegetable Stock (page 19)

¼ cup sugar

2 tablespoons balsamic vinegar

¼ cup dry red wine

1 teaspoon chipotle powder

1 tablespoon New Mexican red chile powder (Chimayo preferred)

1 tablespoon freshly ground white pepper

1 tablespoon ground thyme

1 tablespoon ground marjoram

1 teaspoon ground celery seed

1½ teaspoons ground coriander

2 teaspoons ground cinnamon

1 teaspoon ground ginger

Slices of toasted French bread

Grated Swiss cheese to taste

In a large stockpot, heat the olive oil and add the onion, garlic, mushrooms, parsley, and celery. Sauté until the onions are translucent, about 7 minutes. Add the tomatoes, tomato paste, tomato sauce, vegetable stock, sugar, balsamic vinegar, and the red wine, stirring frequently until the mixture boils.

Add the chipotle powder, red chile powder, white pepper, thyme, marjoram, celery seed, coriander, cinnamon, and ginger and stir well. Reduce the heat to medium and cook for 5 minutes, stirring often.

Place the soup in bowls and top with the French bread slices sprinkled with the cheese. Place the bowls under a broiler until the cheese melts, then serve.

SERVES: 12

# Oyster Mushroom and Thai Chile Herb Soup

HEAT SCALE: HOT

This is a delightful, quick soup to prepare in the light Asian soup tradition. Seldom will you receive such rave comments about a soup this easy to cook. It stores and freezes well—a convenient soup at its best.

3 quarts Vibrant Vegetable Stock (page 19)

1½ teaspoons ground white pepper

1 medium onion, minced

1 teaspoon minced garlic

¼ cup finely chopped celery leaf

8 sprigs parsley, finely chopped

8 oyster mushrooms, stems removed, chopped

4 fresh Thai chiles, or 2 jalapeños or serranos, seeded, stemmed, and minced

Minced cilantro, for garnish

Combine all ingredients in a stockpot and boil for 10 minutes. Serve garnished with the cilantro.

SERVES: 6

# Snappy Snow Pea Soup

Here's a soup from W.C.'s Pacific Rim Meatless class at The Very Best, an Albuquerque cooking school. It is incredibly fast and easy to make, depending almost entirely on the flavor of the fresh snow pea, one of nature's great vegetables. True chileheads can add their favorite Asian hot sauce (such as sriracha) to further inflame this soup. Add firm Japanese silken tofu to make a complete protein soup.

3 quarts water

2 tablespoons sugar

4 tablespoons minced parsley

2 tablespoons minced garlic

4 tablespoons minced green onion

½ cup soy sauce

2 teaspoons ground ginger

4 teaspoons freshly ground white pepper

2 tablespoons chopped watercress

2 tablespoons chopped cilantro

2 cups snow peas, cut diagonally

3 lemons, thinly sliced, for garnish

In a stockpot, combine the water, sugar, parsley, garlic, green onions, soy sauce, ginger, and pepper and boil for 5 minutes. Add the watercress, cilantro, and snow peas and boil 3 more minutes. Transfer the soup to bowls and float the lemon slices on top.

SERVES: 6

# Ethiopian Lentil Soup with Berbere

🔥 🔥 🔥

W.C. likes to use equal amounts of red and yellow lentils for the visual effect. Note that this recipe requires advance preparation.

4 cups dried lentils, washed and soaked in water overnight
3 quarts water
3½ cups chopped red onion
3 tablespoons grated fresh ginger
¼ teaspoon ground nutmeg
½ cup Ethiopian Curried Butter (page 12)
3 tablespoons chopped garlic
1 teaspoon freshly ground black pepper
¼ cup Berbere Paste (page 11)

In a stockpot, combine the lentils and the water and bring to a boil. Cook at a boil, uncovered, stirring occasionally, for 10 minutes.

In a separate pot, combine the remaining ingredients except the Berbere Paste and cook until the onions are soft, about 7 minutes. Add this mixture to the stockpot along with the Berbere Paste, cover, and cook over low heat for 45 minutes, stirring occasionally.

SERVES: 8

NEWSPAPER SOUP (PAGE 43)

CHILLED MANDARIN ORANGE AND
SOUR CHERRY CHILE SOUP (PAGE 93)

WILD MUSHROOM BISQUE WITH
GRILLED CHICKEN (PAGE 35)

# Caribbean Cold and Bold Gazpacho

Heat scale: Medium 🔥 🔥

Traditionally, gazpacho is thought of as a Spanish-style cold soup. However, the cold, uncooked soup idea is taken one step further in this recipe by including some of the fruit bounty available in the Caribbean. The ultimate result is a soup that is cold, bold, and spicy—Island-style.

2 cups pineapple or papaya juice

2 cups tomato juice

¾ cup peeled, chopped papaya

¾ cup coarsely chopped fresh pineapple

⅓ cup diced green pepper

⅓ cup diced red pepper

⅓ cup diced yellow pepper

½ fresh Scotch bonnet chile (or habanero), seeded, stemmed, and minced

3 tablespoons fresh lime juice

2 tablespoons chopped fresh cilantro

½ teaspoon whole black peppercorns, crushed

Place all of the ingredients in a blender and blend for 5 seconds. Refrigerate the mixture for 6 hours.

Serve the soup in icy cold bowls.

SERVES: 4 TO 6

# Chilled African Avocado Soup

This pan-African soup is both cold and hot at the same time. The chiles add the heat, and it is very refreshing in hot weather. The chiles seem to help to cool down the body. Serve it as a first course with fresh crusty bread. We love avocados, and their flavor shines through in this soup.

4 avocados
5 cups Vibrant Vegetable Stock (page 19)
1 tablespoon freshly squeezed lime juice
½ teaspoon salt
¼ teaspoon freshly ground white pepper
3 serrano or jalapeño chiles, seeded, stemmed, and minced
1½ tablespoons minced green onions or chives, for garnish

Mash the avocados in a large bowl. Add the stock, lime juice, salt, pepper, and chiles and continue mashing until the mixture is semi-smooth. If you like a velvety texture, place the mixture in a blender or food processor and purée. Chill the soup for several hours. Garnish the soup with the green onions or chives.

Serves: 4 to 5

# Chilled Mandarin Orange and Sour Cherry Chile Soup

HEAT SCALE: HOT      🔥 🔥 🔥

In a chunkier version, this soup could be a salsa. This is a guaranteed crowd pleaser, both visually and in flavor. The first round of praise comes when it is served, the next when it is tasted. This is one of the favorite soups at W.C.'s Mountain Road Cafe.

3 cups canned mandarin oranges, drained and liquid reserved
1 cup dried sour cherries, rehydrated in the mandarin orange
   liquid
2 medium red bell peppers, diced
2 medium red onions, chopped
3 tablespoons chopped fresh cilantro
4 serrano chiles, seeded, stemmed, and minced
1 teaspoon salt
2 cups freshly squeezed orange juice
1 cup pineapple juice
1 cup coconut milk
1 cup sour cream
¼ teaspoon freshly ground nutmeg

In a large bowl, combine the oranges, sour cherries, peppers, onions, cilantro, chiles, and salt and mix well. Refrigerate for 1 hour. Add the orange juice, pineapple juice, and coconut milk and refrigerate for 30 minutes. Combine the sour cream and the nutmeg and stir well.

    Stir the soup and serve in chilled bowls with a dollop of the sour cream.

SERVES: 6 TO 8

# 6.
# Sizzlin' Stews and Chilis

## Texas Gunpowder Stew

🔥 🔥          HEAT SCALE: MEDIUM

Here's some beef and bean cowboy food, campfire-style. It's not for the faint at heart, featuring ranch beans, sirloin, and Texas gunpowder—better known as jalapeño powder. Serve this with a stout Mexican beer such as Negra Modelo and plenty of warmed tortillas.

3 pounds beef sirloin, trimmed and cut into 1-inch cubes

2 tablespoons vegetable oil

1 tablespoon peanut oil

3 medium onions, chopped

2 tablespoons minced garlic

2½ tablespoons minced fresh parsley

5 very ripe medium tomatoes, coarsely chopped

¼ cup freshly squeezed lime juice

1½ teaspoons ground cumin

2 cups cooked pinto beans

3 okra, finely chopped

1 teaspoon ground cinnamon

½ teaspoon ground bay leaf

8 cups Basic Beef Stock (page 14)

3 tablespoons dried green jalapeño powder

2 tablespoons cider vinegar

Chopped fresh cilantro, for garnish

In a large skillet, brown the beef in the vegetable and peanut oils. Add the onions, garlic, parsley, and tomatoes and sauté until the onions are soft, about 5 minutes. Add the lime juice, cumin, beans, okra, cinnamon, bay leaf, and beef stock and simmer for 1½ to 2 hours. Add water or more beef stock, if needed.

Add the jalapeño powder and simmer for 5 minutes, stirring occasionally. Add the vinegar right before serving and stir well. Garnish with the cilantro and serve.

SERVES: 6

# Border Chile Stew

Serve with a hearty bread and your favorite microbrewed beer.

1 cup chopped New Mexican green chile
1 cup chopped red bell pepper
1 medium onion, chopped
2 tablespoons chopped garlic
2½ tablespoons extra virgin olive oil
3 cups Mountain Road Cafe Classic Chicken Stock (page 15)
2 stalks celery, sliced
2 cups potatoes, cut in ½-inch cubes
1 teaspoon Mexican oregano
1 teaspoon thyme
2 cups cooked pinto beans
6 cups cooked corn kernels
2 cups cooked, chopped chicken
2 cups White Sauce # 1 (page 23)
2 medium zucchinis, chopped
Fried tortilla strips, for garnish

In a stockpot, sauté the chiles, bell pepper, onion, and garlic in the olive oil for 5 to 7 minutes, stirring occasionally. Add the chicken stock, celery, and potatoes and bring to a boil. Reduce the heat, cover, and simmer for 20 minutes, or until the potatoes are tender.

Add the remaining ingredients and enough water to make a thick stew. Simmer over low heat for 15 to 20 minutes. Garnish with the tortilla strips and serve.

Serves: 8 to 10

# Sopapita (Spicy Seafood Stew)

This is one of our favorite stews because it contains so many interesting flavors: coconut milk, allspice, Old Bay, and celery. Serve this with a fruity white wine to bring out the flavor of the spices.

1 quart Traditional European Fish Stock (page 18)
1 tablespoon butter
1 pound sole or any light fish, finely chopped
12 large shrimp, coarsely chopped
12 medium to large whole scallops
1 medium onion, chopped
1 (15-ounce) can Thai coconut milk
2 medium garlic cloves
4 hot chiles, such as chiltepíns, Thai chiles, or piquins, seeded and stemmed
1 teaspoon Old Bay seasoning
¼ teaspoon fresh thyme
1 tablespoon celery leaf
¼ teaspoon freshly ground Jamaican allspice
1½ tablespoons sugar
Lime wedges, for garnish

Heat the fish stock in a large stockpot.

Melt the butter in a sauté pan and lightly sauté the fish, shrimp, and scallops. Remove and reserve.

Combine the remaining ingredients in a food processor and purée. Add the purée to the sauté pan and cook for 5 minutes over medium heat.

Add the reserved seafood and the purée to the fish stock, stirring well. Cook over low heat for 15 minutes. Garnish with the lime wedges and serve hot.

SERVES: 4

# New Mexican Green Chile Stew

☙ ☙                    HEAT SCALE: MEDIUM

This is a dish with as many variations as there are cooks—and each one thinks his or hers is the finest. It is a basic staple of New Mexican cookery and is prepared and cooked in its own category in Southwestern chili cook-offs. Serve corn or flour tortillas with this stew. Sometimes chopped raw onions and chopped fresh Mexican oregano are served as a garnish.

2 pounds lean pork, cubed

2 tablespoons vegetable oil

1 large onion, chopped

2 cloves garlic, minced

6 to 8 green New Mexican chiles, roasted, peeled, seeded, stemmed, and chopped

1 large potato, peeled and diced (optional)

2 tomatoes, peeled and chopped

3 cups water or Basic Beef Stock (page 14)

Brown the pork in the oil. Add the onion and garlic and sauté for 2 minutes.

Place the pork, onion, garlic, and the remaining ingredients in a stockpot. Cover and simmer for 1½ to 2 hours, or until the meat is very tender.

SERVES: 6

# Black Bean Corned Beef Chile Stew

HEAT SCALE: MILD

Corned beef in a stew? Why not experiment? You can either prepare your own corned beef or purchase it from the butcher. You'll find this a delightful mix of flavors and easy to make; just be sure to skim off any fat that comes to the surface. Serve it with an Irish soda bread accompanied by a black and tan beer.

3 quarts water

2½ pounds corned beef

2 carrots, peeled and chopped

1 large onion, chopped

½ bunch parsley, chopped

1 teaspoon salt

1 tablespoon freshly ground black pepper

1 tablespoon freshly ground white pepper

2 cups W.C.'s Green Chile Sauce (page 26)

3 cups cooked black beans

Combine all ingredients in a stockpot and boil uncovered for 2 hours. Remove the corned beef, trim the fat, and set aside. Strain the soup and discard all solids, then skim the fat. Shred the corned beef, cut into 1½-inch lengths and return to the soup. Add enough water to make about a gallon. Heat to boiling, stir well, and serve hot.

SERVES: 8 TO 10

# Garbanzo and Chorizo Stew

Here is our version of a classic Spanish stew, heated up with the addition of spicy chorizo and red chile pods. Note that the garbanzo beans require advance preparation unless you buy them canned. Serve this with a hard, crusty bread such as the Spanish *bolillos*.

3 quarts water

1 pound dried garbanzo beans, soaked in water overnight, or
  2 (15-ounce) cans

3 tablespoons chopped garlic

1 medium onion, chopped

6 sprigs parsley, chopped

3 whole bay leaves

1 tablespoon salt

1 tablespoon freshly ground black pepper

1 pound chorizo sausage, cut into 1-inch slices

3 whole red New Mexican chiles, seeded and stemmed

1 pound fresh spinach, washed well and coarsely chopped

1 pound baby Red Bliss potatoes, cut in half

In a large stockpot, combine the water, garbanzo beans, garlic, onion, parsley, bay leaves, salt, black pepper, chorizo, and chiles and bring to a boil. Reduce heat, cover, and simmer for 2 hours. If using canned garbanzo beans, simmer for 30 minutes.

Remove from the heat, skim the fat from the stew, and add the spinach, potatoes, and water as needed. Cook over medium heat for 30 minutes, stirring often, or until the potatoes are tender. Remove and discard the chile pods before serving.

Serves: 8

# Caribbean Pepper Pot Soup

There are dozens of variations of this soup (actually a stew) throughout the Caribbean. If you talk to a dozen people, you'll get a dozen different recipes, with each person claiming theirs is the only way to create the perfect pepper pot soup! We present to you a rather basic recipe, utilizing the ingredients that most cooks will agree upon. Please embellish it so that *you* have the best pepper pot soup.

2 cups chopped onion

½ pound diced salt pork, rind removed, or 1 salted pig's tail

2 cloves garlic, minced

1 teaspoon dried thyme

7 cups water

1 pound callaloo or spinach, chopped

½ pound white potatoes, peeled and diced into ½-inch cubes

½ pound yams, peeled and diced into ½-inch cubes

1 large fresh Scotch bonnet chile (or habanero), seeded, stemmed, and minced

2 tablespoons vegetable oil

12 small okras, washed and sliced

1½ cups coconut milk

1 cup cooked, chopped shrimp

Salt and pepper to taste

Place the onion, salt pork, garlic, thyme, and water into a large, heavy stockpot. Bring the mixture to a boil, skim any froth that rises to the surface in the first 4 to 5 minutes of boiling, then reduce the heat to a simmer. Cover and cook for 1 hour.

Add the callaloo, potatoes, yams, and chile to the soup and bring back to a boil. Reduce the heat to a simmer, cover, and cook for 45 minutes.

Heat the vegetable oil in a skillet. Sauté the sliced okra until they are lightly browned, about 2 minutes, and add them to the soup. Simmer the soup for 5 more minutes, or until the okra is tender.

Stir the coconut milk and the shrimp into the soup and let it simmer 5 minutes, stirring occasionally. Season with salt and pepper.

Serve the soup in heated bowls.

SERVES: 8

# Ethiopian Chicken Stew

This recipe, known as *doro we't*, is considered to be the national dish of Ethiopia. W.C. was taught this recipe by some Ethiopian friends in Rehoboth Beach, Delaware. When they found out that he loved hot and spicy foods, they were eager to give it to him. Traditionally served with native *injera* bread, we recommend any unleavened bread (such as pita or lahvosh) as a substitute.

3- to 4-pound chicken, quartered

¼ cup lemon juice

1 tablespoon salt

1½ cups minced onion

¼ cup Ethiopian Curried Butter (page 12)

1½ cups minced garlic

1½ teaspoons freshly grated ginger

¼ teaspoon ground fenugreek seeds

¼ teaspoon ground nutmeg

¼ teaspoon ground cardamom

¼ cup Berbere Paste (page 11)

1 tablespoon Hungarian paprika

¾ teaspoon ground black pepper

¼ cup dry white wine

¾ cup water

8 hard-boiled eggs

1 quart Mountain Road Cafe Classic Chicken Stock (page 15)

Rub the chicken with the lemon juice and sprinkle the salt over it. Set aside.

Add the onion to a heavy stockpot and cook over medium heat for 5 minutes, stirring constantly to avoid burning. Stir in the butter and continue cooking for 2 minutes, stirring constantly. Add the garlic, ginger, fenugreek, nutmeg, and cardamom and stir well. Add the Berbere Paste, paprika, and black pepper, stirring often, and cook for 3 minutes. Stir in the wine and water and bring to a boil for 3 minutes until thickened.

Add the chicken and toss to coat. Reduce the heat to low, cover, and cook for 15 minutes. Peel the eggs and puncture the surfaces with a fork. Add the eggs to the pot, cover, and cook 15 more minutes.

Remove the chicken, cool, and debone. Return the chicken to the pot, add the stock, and heat, stirring often.

To serve, place a whole egg in each bowl and spoon in the rest of the soup. Alternately, the eggs can be chopped and sprinkled over the chicken stew.

SERVES: 8

# Caldo Puchero
# (Pot of Vegetable Stew
# with Chiltepíns)

HEAT SCALE: HOT

Like most stews, this one takes a while to cook, about 4 hours. It is interesting because it contains a number of pre-Columbian ingredients, namely chiltepíns, corn, squash, potatoes, and tepary beans. The spicy heat can be adjusted by adding or subtracting chiltepíns.

15 chiltepíns, or more to taste
1 beef soup bone with marrow

1 cup dried tepary or garbanzo beans

4 cloves garlic, chopped

1 acorn or butternut squash, peeled, seeded, and cut into
   1-inch cubes

3 ears corn, cut into 2-inch rounds

4 carrots, peeled and cut into 1-inch pieces

1 head cabbage, quartered

3 green New Mexican chiles, roasted, peeled, seeded,
   stemmed, and chopped

3 stalks celery, cut into 1-inch pieces

2 potatoes or sweet potatoes, cut into 1-inch cubes

3 zucchini, cut into ½-inch slices

1 onion, quartered

2 cups fresh string beans, cut into 1-inch pieces

½ cup minced cilantro

In a large stockpot, combine the chiltepíns, soup bone, tepary or garbanzo beans, garlic, and water as needed to cover. Bring to a boil,
reduce heat, and simmer for 1 hour.

Add the acorn or butternut squash, the corn, and 1 quart of
water and simmer for 30 minutes.

Add the carrots and cabbage and simmer for 15 minutes.

Add the chiles, celery, and potatoes or sweet potatoes and cook
for 30 minutes.

Add the zucchini, onion, and string beans and simmer for 30 to
45 minutes, or until everything is tender. When ready to serve,
remove the soup bone and add the cilantro.

SERVES: 8

# Sopa de Lima, Peru

When is a stew not a stew? When it's cooked like a stew and served like a broth. This stew-soup is a favorite in Lima, the capital of Peru. It is different from the Yucatan soup of the same name that features the Key lime. The rocoto, the favorite chile in this recipe, was a principal crop of the Inca society in Peru, and centuries later is still the chile of choice. Cooks will have to grow their own or substitute jalapeños; however, persons living near the Mexican border can often find the rocoto's close relatives, called canarios, in markets in cities such as Ciudad Juárez.

4 quarts water (or more if necessary)

2 pounds beef brisket, flank, or short ribs

1 whole onion

1 whole tomato

½ cup dried garbanzo beans

Bouquet garni: 2 sprigs parsley, 1 sprig fresh rosemary, 2 sprigs fresh thyme, 4 whole black peppercorns, tied in cheesecloth

1 rocoto or jalapeño chile, whole

1 teaspoon salt

6 carrots, cut into ½-inch pieces

3 turnips, peeled and cut into ½-inch cubes

2 ears corn, cut into 2-inch rounds

1 small yucca, peeled and cut into ½-inch cubes (optional)

3 potatoes, cut into ½-inch cubes

1 cabbage, cut into eighths

3 leeks, white part only, sliced into ½-inch pieces

1 celery rib, cut into ½-inch pieces

1 tablespoon cooking oil

1 cup sliced onion

½ cup sliced rocoto chiles or jalapeños

Salt and pepper to taste

Heat the water in a large stockpot. When the water is warm, add the beef, onion, tomato, garbanzo beans, and the bouquet garni. Bring the water to a boil, reduce heat, and simmer for ½ hour.

Remove the onion and tomato, press through a fine sieve, and return the purée to the pot. Add the whole chile and cook for an additional 1½ hours.

Add the salt, carrots, turnips, corn, yucca, potatoes, cabbage, leeks, and celery and simmer until the vegetables are tender, 20 to 30 minutes.

Remove the meat to a platter. Remove the vegetables with a slotted spoon and arrange them around the meat. Keep warm in the oven.

For the sauce, heat the oil and sauté the onion and chiles until the onion is translucent. Add salt and pepper.

Serve the broth first in soup bowls, followed by the meat and vegetables covered with the sauce.

SERVES: 6 TO 8

# Curried Chicken and Banana Stew

HEAT SCALE: MEDIUM

This dish, known as *supu ya n dizi*, is from Tanzania, East Africa, and shows an Indian influence.

4 pounds of chicken pieces

3 tablespoons peanut oil

3 cloves garlic, minced

1 cup chopped onion

2 cups chopped celery

2½ tablespoons hot Madras curry powder

1½ teaspoons salt

1 teaspoon freshly ground black pepper

1 tablespoon ground or crushed red chile

2 cups chopped tomato

1 cup shredded coconut

1½ quarts Mountain Road Cafe Classic Chicken Stock (page 15)

2 slightly underripe bananas, peeled and sliced

In a large, heavy stockpot, brown the chicken in the oil. Drain the chicken on paper towels and set aside.

Sauté the garlic, onion, and celery in the remaining oil for 1 minute. Add the curry powder, salt, black pepper, and red chile and sauté for 1 minute.

Add the chicken, tomato, coconut, and chicken stock. Bring the mixture to a boil. Reduce the heat to a simmer, cover and cook for 40 minutes, until the chicken is very tender.

Debone the chicken, return it to the pan, and add the bananas. Simmer for 10 minutes.

SERVES: 6

# W.C.'s Green Chili

This recipe is meatless and dairyless and is easily frozen or canned. A third-generation New Mexican told W.C., "It's a shame when your favorite green chili is made by a transplanted Anglo."

6 cups chopped New Mexican green chiles
1 clove garlic, minced
1 medium onion, coarsely chopped
⅛ teaspoon ground coriander
½ tablespoon red chile powder
½ teaspoon ground white pepper
½ teaspoon cumin powder
1 tablespoon salt
11½ cups water
2 tablespoons cornstarch

In a large stockpot, combine the green chiles, garlic, onion, coriander, chile powder, pepper, cumin, salt, and 10 cups water. Bring to a boil and boil, uncovered, for 1 hour.

In a small bowl, combine the cornstarch and the remaining 1½ cups water and mix thoroughly. Add to the chile mixture and cook until the mixture clears, about 20 minutes.

YIELD: ABOUT 12 CUPS

# Cincinnati-Style Chili

This chili is often served over pasta and is then called chili-mac or two-way chili. For best results, cook macaroni or penne pasta al dente, cover with chili, and top with grated Parmesan cheese.

2 pounds coarsely ground chuck steak

1 quart water

1 cup chopped onions

2 (8-ounce) cans tomato sauce

4 cloves garlic, minced

¼ teaspoon ground allspice

4 whole cloves, crushed

1 bay leaf, crushed

½ ounce unsweetened chocolate

3 tablespoons chile powder (or more to taste)

2 tablespoons cider vinegar

2 teaspoons Worcestershire sauce

½ teaspoon salt

1 teaspoon ground cumin

1 teaspoon ground cinnamon

1½ teaspoons sugar

2 tablespoons flour mixed with ¼ cup water

Combine the chuck steak and the water in a large stockpot and simmer for 30 minutes. Add the remaining ingredients except the flour mixed with water and simmer for 3 hours.

Add the flour mixed with water, bring to a boil, and cook for 5 minutes. Remove from the heat and serve.

SERVES: 6

# Short Rib Chili

This chili recipe, one of Dave's favorites, was invented by his wife, Mary Jane. It is easy to make, cooks in 2½ hours, and combines the best of both red and green chiles. Serve it with corn bread and a big green salad.

4 pounds beef short ribs

2 tablespoons corn oil

1 onion, chopped

1 green bell pepper, chopped

2 cloves garlic, chopped

2 cups Basic Beef Stock (page 14)

2 tablespoons New Mexican red chile powder (Chimayo preferred)

1 (12-ounce) can stewed tomatoes, crushed

1 cup chopped New Mexican green chiles

3½ cups cooked kidney beans, pinto beans, or black beans, drained

2 cups cooked fresh corn, cut off the cob

Trim the excess fat from the short ribs. Heat the oil in a large stock-pot and brown the ribs. Add the onion, bell pepper, and garlic and sauté for 1 minute. Add the beef stock.

Add the remaining ingredients, except the beans and corn, and bring to a boil. Reduce the heat to a simmer. Cover and cook for 2½ hours, stirring occasionally.

Just before serving, add the corn and the beans and heat through. For convenience, you may want to cut the meat off the bones.

SERVES: 8

# U.B. Alarmed Five-Chile Chili

This is an unusual chili that could also be termed a stew. This is not for beginning chileheads but for the serious aficionado. The name was inspired by the heat scales of most other weaker chilis. W.C. has taken some grief over the addition of turnips and potatoes here, but the results defend him. In case it's too hot, serve this with milk or beer.

7 cups Basic Beef Stock (page 14)

1 tablespoon minced garlic

4 small carrots, peeled and sliced into ¼-inch rounds

1½ tablespoons minced fresh parsley

½ teaspoon ground cumin

½ tablespoon dried Mexican oregano

½ teaspoon cinnamon

1 pound turnips, peeled and coarsely shredded

2 pounds potatoes, peeled and cut into ½-inch cubes

2 tablespoons vegetable shortening

1 medium onion, chopped

1 pound ground beef

1½ cups canned crushed tomatoes

½ cup apple cider

3 tablespoons tomato paste

½ cup browned butter roux (½ cup flour browned in ¼ cup butter)

3 large dried chipotle chiles

½ cup Jack Daniels bourbon (Black Label)

1 teaspoon salt

6 chiles de árbol (or any small, hot, dried red chiles), seeded, stemmed, and crushed

¾ teaspoon ground habanero chile

1 large mirasol or New Mexican chile, seeded, stemmed, and crushed

8 chiltepíns or piquín chiles, crushed

3 tablespoons olive oil

3 tablespoons red wine vinegar

6 tablespoons raw or dark honey

Sour cream, for garnish

Chopped green onions, for garnish

In a stockpot, combine the stock, garlic, carrots, parsley, cumin, oregano, cinnamon, turnips, and potatoes and bring to a boil. Boil, uncovered, for 20 minutes, adding water as needed.

In a large skillet, heat the shortening, add the onion and sauté for 5 minutes. Add the beef and cook until browned. Add the tomatoes, apple cider, tomato paste, and roux and simmer, uncovered, stirring occasionally, for 10 minutes. Remove from the heat and reserve.

Rehydrate the chipotles in the bourbon for 45 minutes, using a bowl to keep them submerged. Combine the chipotles in a food processor or blender with the remaining ingredients and purée. Add this purée to the meat mixture and stir well. Add the meat mixture to the boiling soup and mix well. Reduce the heat and simmer for 10 minutes before serving. Garnish with the sour cream and green onions.

SERVES: 10 TO 12

# New Mexican Venison Cauldron

Halfway between a chili and a stew, this recipe is one of the best uses for venison that we've found. (The venison is marinated in both red and green chile.) Note that this recipe requires advance preparation. Since this is a variation on hunter's stew, W.C. suggests serving it with biscuits. We've substituted ostrich meat for the venison with good results.

1 venison roast, 3½ to 4 pounds, cut into 1½-inch cubes
1½ teaspoons salt
2 tablespoons New Mexican red chile powder (Chimayo preferred)
2 cups W.C.'s Green Chile Sauce (page 26)
1½ teaspoons minced garlic
2 tablespoons red wine vinegar
2 medium onions, diced
5 cups Mountain Road Cafe Classic Chicken Stock (page 15)
2 medium stalks celery, chopped
2 medium carrots, peeled and cut into ½-inch rounds
6 medium potatoes, peeled and cut into 1-inch cubes
2 medium rutabagas, peeled and cut into ¾-inch cubes
1 teaspoon crushed black peppercorns

In a shallow baking dish, toss the venison cubes with the salt and chile powder. In a bowl, combine the green chile sauce, garlic, and red wine vinegar and pour this over the venison. Marinate for at least 1 hour.

In a large stockpot, add the onions and cook over medium heat for 2 minutes, stirring constantly. Add the chicken stock, celery, carrots, potatoes, rutabagas, black pepper, and the venison with the

marinade and simmer, uncovered, for 2 hours, adding water as needed to maintain the liquid.

SERVES: 8 TO 10


# Southwest Ham and Pinto Bean Stew

HEAT SCALE: MEDIUM

Anasazi beans may be substituted for the pinto beans in this recipe.
Note that this recipe requires advance preparation. It is important
to buy a high-quality ham; if it's bone-in, save the bone for another
project.

2 cups pinto beans, soaked overnight in water

1 quart water

1 quart Mountain Road Cafe Classic Chicken Stock (page 15)

3 medium onions, chopped

3 large cloves garlic, minced

¼ cup green bell pepper, coarsely chopped

2 tablespoons red chile powder (Chimayo preferred)

1 teaspoon salt

1 teaspoon dried Mexican oregano

½ teaspoon ground dried rosemary

½ teaspoon dried thyme

½ teaspoon ground basil

½ teaspoon ground cloves

1 tablespoon minced fresh parsley

2 tablespoons dark brown sugar

1 teaspoon crushed bay leaf

½ teaspoon ground cumin

½ teaspoon ground celery seed

½ teaspoon ground marjoram

1 teaspoon curry powder

1 tablespoon ground white pepper

1 pound diced smoked ham

1 cup dry Spanish sherry

Diced onions, for garnish

Minced pickled jalapeño chiles, for garnish

In a stockpot, combine all ingredients except the sherry and garnishes. Bring to a boil for 5 minutes, then reduce the heat and simmer, uncovered, until the beans are soft, about 1½ hours. Immediately before serving, add the sherry and stir well. Serve sprinkled with the onions and minced jalapeños.

SERVES: 8

# 7.
# Pyrotechnic Pan-Asian Pots

## Lemongrass-Gingered Chicken Wonton Soup

HEAT SCALE: MEDIUM

This is our first of several wonton soups. You can buy ground chicken from your butcher, but be sure to specify that the skin should be removed before grinding. Or you can use a food processor fitted with a sharp blade and chop your own chicken, using the pulse mode to get the proper consistency. Serve this with a cold Tsingtao beer.

1 pound ground chicken (dark meat preferred)

½ cup finely chopped spinach leaves

1½ tablespoons sherry

1 tablespoon soy sauce

1 teaspoon ground ginger

¼ cup shredded fresh ginger

2 stalks lemongrass, minced

1½ tablespoons finely chopped fresh Asian or serrano chiles

40 to 50 prepared wonton skins

3 quarts Wonton Soup Broth (page 17)

Peanut oil

Chopped parsley, for garnish

Combine the chicken, spinach, sherry, soy sauce, ground ginger, fresh ginger, lemongrass, and chiles in a bowl, mix well, and let sit for 30 minutes. Spoon 1 teaspoon of the filling onto a wonton skin, fold the skin over and press firmly to seal. Continue until the filling is gone.

Heat the broth in a stockpot.

Heat the peanut oil in a wok and fry the wontons in batches until golden brown, about 7 to 9 minutes. Remove to a paper towel and drain.

Place 4 or 5 wontons in each soup bowl, ladle the broth over, and garnish with the parsley.

SERVES: 8 TO 10

# Duck and Asian Pear Wonton Soup

 HEAT SCALE: MEDIUM

Asian pears are found from Korea to Thailand and have less sugar and juice than other pears. If you're going to substitute, use an unripe pear. Garnish by floating very thin slices of the beautiful star fruit on top.

1 pound ground duck breast

1 teaspoon five-spice powder

1 tablespoon honey

1 tablespoon teriyaki sauce

3 fresh Thai or serrano chiles, seeded, stemmed, and minced

1 tablespoon dark brown sugar

1½ tablespoons freshly squeezed lemon juice

½ teaspoon salt

½ teaspoon finely ground white pepper

¼ teaspoon vanilla

2 Asian pears, peeled and grated

½ cup finely shredded red cabbage

1 tablespoon sherry

1 tablespoon soy sauce

40 to 50 wonton skins

3 quarts Wonton Soup Broth (page 17)

Peanut oil

Chopped cilantro, for garnish

In a large bowl, combine the duck, five-spice powder, honey, teriyaki, chiles, brown sugar, lemon juice, salt, pepper, and vanilla. Mix well and let sit for 30 minutes. Add the pears, cabbage, sherry, and soy sauce, mix well, and let sit another 30 minutes. Drain as much of the liquid from the filling as possible and discard.

Spoon 1 teaspoon of the filling onto a wonton skin, fold the skin over and press firmly to seal. Continue until the filling is gone.

Heat the broth in a stockpot.

Heat the peanut oil in a wok and fry the wontons in batches until golden brown, about 7 to 9 minutes. Remove to a paper towel and drain.

Place 4 or 5 wontons in each soup bowl, ladle the broth over, and garnish with the cilantro.

SERVES: 8 TO 10

# Apricot, Crab, and Chile Wonton Soup

If you want to wow your crowd, this soup will do it! It's a nice blending of subtle flavors with a slight blast of heat from the chile powder. Serve this with a well-chilled Japanese plum wine.

½ cup apricot preserves

1 tablespoon brandy

½ teaspoon dry mustard

½ cup finely shredded white cabbage

¼ cup finely chopped bok choy

4 green onions, minced

½ cup whole mung bean sprouts

¾ teaspoon ground ginger

2 tablespoons hot red chile powder

1 pound crabmeat, well cleaned

3 tablespoons bottled oyster sauce

1¼ tablespoons minced garlic

2 tablespoons hot chile oil

40 to 50 wonton skins

3 quarts Wonton Soup Broth (page 17)

Peanut oil

Chopped parsley, for garnish

In a bowl, combine the preserves, brandy, mustard, cabbage, bok choy, green onions, sprouts, ginger, chile, crabmeat, oyster sauce, garlic, and chile oil, mix well and let sit for 1 hour. Drain as much of the liquid from the filling as possible and discard.

    Spoon 1 teaspoon of the filling onto a wonton skin, fold the skin over and press firmly to seal. Continue until the filling is gone.

Heat the broth in a pot.

Heat the peanut oil in a wok and fry the wontons in batches until golden brown, about 7 to 9 minutes. Remove to a paper towel and drain.

Place 4 or 5 wontons in each soup bowl, ladle the broth over, and garnish with the parsley.

SERVES: 8 TO 10

# Thai Fish Chowder with Shrimp Wontons

HEAT SCALE: MEDIUM

We love Thai foods that combine lemongrass with the citrus flavor of lime leaves and the unique taste of fish sauce. Galangal is a gingerlike root from the Far East (particularly Indonesia and Malaysia) that you may be able to find in an Asian market. (If not, you may substitute ginger.) The flavor is similar to ginger but with added hints of pine and citrus. This is one of W.C.'s favorite soups to serve at the Mountain Road Cafe, and one of Dave's favorites to eat there.

1 egg
20 medium shrimp
1 teaspoon five-spice powder
½ teaspoon sesame oil
1 tablespoon bread crumbs
24 wonton skins
½ cup vegetable oil
3 tablespoons crushed garlic
1 onion, chopped
2 quarts Wonton Soup Broth (page 17)

1 tablespoon coarsely ground white pepper

2 lemongrass stalks, white part only, cut into rings

2 (1-inch) pieces galangal, peeled

6 Thai chiles, or 3 serranos or jalapeños, seeded, stemmed, and sliced

6 kaffir lime leaves or zest of ½ lime

¾ pound rock shrimp, peeled

½ pounds crabmeat or sole, coarsely chopped

½ cup straw mushrooms

½ cup chopped baby corn

6 tablespoons fish sauce (Tiparos brand recommended)

6 tablespoons freshly squeezed lime juice

1 teaspoon sugar

5 to 6 tablespoons coarsely chopped cilantro, for garnish

Combine the egg, shrimp, five-spice powder, sesame oil, and bread crumbs in a food processor and coarsely purée. Spoon 1 teaspoon of the filling onto a wonton skin, fold the skin over and press firmly to seal. Continue until the filling is gone.

Heat ¼ cup of the vegetable oil in a wok and fry the wontons in batches until they are golden brown, about 7 to 9 minutes. Remove to a paper towel and drain. Reserve the wontons.

In a large stockpot, heat the remaining ¼ cup oil and sauté the garlic and onion for 3 minutes. Add the broth and bring to a boil, stirring occasionally. Add the white pepper, lemongrass, galangal, chiles, lime leaves, shrimp, crab, straw mushrooms, and baby corn and boil for 3 minutes. Add the remaining ingredients and boil for 3 minutes. Remove and discard the galangal pieces and kaffir lime leaves. Place 3 wontons in each bowl and ladle the chowder over them, then garnish with the cilantro.

SERVES: 8

# Hong Kong Chestnut Soup

W.C. invented this soup in Hong Kong when he smelled the wok-roasted chestnuts being cooked by street vendors and thought about using them in unique ways. This is a rich, heavily textured soup that can stand alone.

2 cups peeled chestnuts

1 quart water

3 tablespoons peanut oil

1 cup minced bok choy

2 teaspoons finely chopped leeks, white part only

1½ cups cooked, mashed black beans

2 quarts Mountain Road Cafe Classic Chicken Stock (page 15)

1 cup diced cooked hot Chinese sausage

1 tablespoon finely chopped fresh parsley

1 teaspoon salt

1 teaspoon soy sauce

2 tablespoons rice flour

1 cup coconut milk

1 teaspoon sherry

Asian garlic-chile sauce

In a stockpot, combine the chestnuts and water over high heat and boil until the chestnuts are soft, about 20 minutes. Drain the chestnuts and mash them.

In another pot, heat the peanut oil until hot, add the bok choy and leeks and cook for 8 minutes. Add the beans, chestnuts, chicken stock, sausage, parsley, salt, and soy sauce and bring to a boil.

In a bowl, combine the rice flour and coconut milk. Add this to the soup and stir with a whisk to thicken. Turn off the heat, add the sherry, stir well, and serve. Serve the Asian garlic-chile sauce on the side for your guests to add heat as they like.

SERVES: 6 TO 8

# Vietnamese Sweet and Sour Snapper Soup

### HEAT SCALE: VARIES

This soup, known as *cahn chua ca*, is very representative of many of the soups of Vietnam. It is delicately seasoned, and one ingredient doesn't overwhelm the other; instead, all the ingredients present a balanced taste in this easy and quick-to-prepare recipe. Once again, we see that snapper is ubiquitous all over the world.

1 pound snapper or other delicate whitefish fillets

3 tablespoons frozen orange juice

1½ tablespoons apple cider vinegar

1 medium onion, thinly sliced

1 quart water

3 medium tomatoes, peeled and sliced

1½ cups mung bean sprouts

1⅓ cups thinly sliced celery

1 teaspoon soy sauce

Freshly ground black pepper to taste

¼ teaspoon ground cayenne

2 tablespoons chopped cilantro

Fresh red serrano or jalapeño slices to taste

Rinse the fish fillets with cold water and dry with paper towels. Cut the fish into 1-inch pieces and set aside.

In a large saucepan, combine the orange juice, vinegar, onion, and water and bring to a boil. Cover the pan and simmer gently for 15 minutes.

Add the tomatoes to the simmering water and continue to cook for 3 to 4 minutes, or until the tomatoes begin to soften.

Stir in the fish and the remaining ingredients and simmer for 2 minutes.

SERVES: 4

# Macau Pork and Clam Soup

HEAT SCALE: VARIES

W.C. discovered this recipe during a visit to a waterfront restaurant in Macau. The chef, a man in his sixties, learned it from his grand-father. The recipe incorporates both Chinese and Portuguese elements. Note that this recipe requires advance preparation. Serve garnished with lemon wedges and with a hard, crusty bread for dipping.

1½ pounds pork butt, well trimmed and cut into 1-inch cubes
2 tablespoons minced garlic
1 tablespoon Piri-Piri Sauce (page 25), plus additional for garnish
2 cups dry white wine
½ teaspoon finely ground black pepper
1½ teaspoons salt
¼ teaspoon ground bay leaf
¼ cup extra virgin olive oil
1½ tablespoons Spanish paprika

3 medium red onions, sliced thinly and then coarsely chopped

2 pounds well-scrubbed baby clams in shells

1 cup Mountain Road Cafe Classic Chicken Stock (page 15)

2 cups Traditional European Fish Stock (page 18)

6 cups water

In a large bowl, combine the pork, garlic, 1 tablespoon of Piri-Piri Sauce, wine, pepper, salt, and bay leaf and marinate for 3 hours. Remove the pork, drain on paper towels, and reserve the marinade.

Heat 2 tablespoons of the olive oil in a large, heavy stockpot and brown the pork over medium heat. Add the reserved marinade and paprika and simmer for 30 minutes. Skim off any fat.

In a separate stockpot, heat the remaining olive oil, add the onions, and sauté over medium heat for 5 minutes, stirring frequently. Add the clams and cover for 2 minutes. Add the stock, water, and the pork and cook over medium heat for 5 minutes, stirring often. Serve with Piri-Piri Sauce on the side, if desired, for additional heat.

SERVES: 6 TO 8

# Spicy Macau Bean Stew with Sausage and Ham

HEAT SCALE: MEDIUM

This is one of the more unusual stews—a very hearty and satisfying meal both for the palate and the appetite. Note that this recipe requires advance preparation. Serve with an ice cold Tsingtao beer or a lusty red wine, like Chianti.

1 cup navy beans, soaked overnight

1 cup kidney beans, soaked overnight

2 quarts water

1 cup diced cooked ham

½ cup chopped red bell pepper

½ cup chopped green bell pepper

½ cup diced carrots

¾ cup chopped cabbage

2 medium potatoes, peeled and diced

1 medium onion, finely chopped

1½ tablespoons minced garlic

2 medium tomatoes, peeled, seeded, and diced

2 teaspoons tomato paste

4 cups Mountain Road Cafe Classic Chicken Stock (page 15)

1 teaspoon crushed black peppercorns

½ teaspoon dried thyme

2 teaspoons salt

½ pound linguica (Portuguese garlic sausage) or kielbasa, cut into thin rounds

½ cup cooked small pasta shells

2 tablespoons Piri-Piri Sauce (page 25)

In a stockpot, combine the beans, water, ham, bell peppers, carrots, cabbage, potatoes, onion, garlic, and tomatoes and cook, uncovered, over medium heat for 15 minutes.

Add the tomato paste, chicken stock, peppercorns, thyme, and salt, reduce the heat, and simmer, covered, for 2½ hours, stirring frequently.

Add the sausage, pasta shells, and Piri-Piri Sauce and cook for 10 minutes on low heat, stirring constantly. Check for spiciness and add more Piri-Piri Sauce if necessary.

SERVES: 8 TO 10

# Chinese Tortilla Soup

HEAT SCALE: MEDIUM  🔥 🔥

Wonton skins are the "tortillas" in this quick and easy Asian soup. W.C. was suffering jet lag when he created this recipe in Hong Kong and didn't realize where he was! He insists that you serve this with a French brandy sour. Incidentally, people in Hong Kong consume more French brandy than the residents of Paris.

2 tablespoons peanut oil

8 wonton skins, cut into ¼-inch-by-2½-inch pieces

2 fresh Asian chiles or serrano or jalapeño chiles, seeded, stemmed, and chopped

1 large leek, cleaned well, green part discarded, julienned into strips ¼ inch by 2 inches

3 cloves garlic, minced

¼ teaspoon ground ginger

¼ teaspoon five-spice powder

½ teaspoon sugar

2 teaspoons black bean paste

5 cups Vibrant Vegetable Stock (page 19) or Mountain Road Cafe Classic Chicken Stock (page 15)

3 tablespoons minced cilantro, for garnish

In a wok or skillet, heat the peanut oil until very hot and toss the wonton strips until they are crisp. Remove and blot on paper towels. Line 4 soup bowls with the skins and set aside.

In a stockpot, combine the remaining ingredients except the cilantro and bring to a boil. Reduce the heat and simmer, uncovered, for 10 minutes. Pour the soup into the bowls and garnish with the cilantro.

SERVES: 4

# Cream of Ginger Soup
# with Lemongrass

We love this combination of flavors because of the distinctive lemongrass. Note that this soup is flavored only with herbs and has no meat, poultry, or fish in it. (If you find this soup is too mild, add ½ teaspoon habanero powder to the roux.) When you're entertaining and don't know the palate preferences of all your guests, serve this soup!

3 tablespoons Sichuan chile oil

⅔ cup butter or margarine

1 cup sifted all-purpose flour

1 teaspoon salt

1 teaspoon ground ginger

1 teaspoon minced shallot

½ teaspoon white pepper

2 stalks lemongrass, white part only, cut into rings

2 cups Vibrant Vegetable Stock (page 19)

2 tablespoons grated ginger

2 quarts milk

2 cups heavy cream

3 tablespoons white wine

1½ tablespoons sugar

In a large saucepan, heat the oil and butter over medium heat. With a whisk, whip in the flour, salt, ginger, shallot, white pepper, and lemongrass until smooth to make a roux. Do not brown. Remove from the heat and set aside.

In a stockpot, bring the stock to a boil. Add the ginger, milk, and cream and bring to a boil. Reduce the heat, add the wine and sugar, and stir well.

Return the roux to medium heat to warm it and with a whisk, whip it into the heated milk mixture until all is well blended and smooth. Adjust the consistency with more milk if necessary and serve hot.

SERVES: 8

# Index

Sweet and Hot Pepper Consommé, 27
Sweet and Spicy Lobster Tail Soup,
   66–67
Sweet Potato Chipotle Chile Bisque,
   48–49

T

Texas Gunpowder Stew, 94–95
Thai Fish Chowder with Shrimp
   Wontons, 121–22
Tomatoes. *See also* Chilis
   Basque-Style Bonito Tomato
      Chowder, 60–61
   Caribbean Cold and Bold Gazpacho,
      91
   Chipotle Tomato Soup con Queso,
      86–87
   Cream of Roma Tomato Soup with
      Jalapeños, 46
   Striped Bass Bouillabaisse with
      Rouille, 54–55
   Sweet and Hot Pepper Consommé,
      27
   Tomato-Orange Ginger Soup, 28
Tortillas
   Gulf of Mexico Seafood Tortilla
      Soup, 32–33
   White and Blue Tortilla Chili, 72–73
Traditional European Fish Stock, 18
Turnip Soup, Cream of, with Garlic
   and Habanero, 77–78

U

U.B. Alarmed Five-Chile Chili, 112–13

V

Vegetables. *See also individual*
   *vegetables*
   Caldo Puchero (Pot of Vegetable
      Stew with Chiltepíns), 104–5

Double Chile Vegetarian Stew,
   78–79
New Mexican Venison Cauldron,
   114–15
Sopa de Lima, Peru, 106–7
Vibrant Vegetable Stock, 19–20
Wild Mushroom and Vegetable
   Gumbo with Jalapeños, 76–77
Venison Cauldron, New Mexican,
   114–15
Veracruz-Style Shrimp Chowder, 56
Vibrant Vegetable Stock, 19–20
Vietnamese Sweet and Sour Snapper
   Soup, 124–25

W

W.C.'s Chimayo Red Chile Sauce, 29
W.C.'s Double Clam Rio Grande
   Chowder, 68–69
W.C.'s Green Chile Sauce, 26
W.C.'s Green Chili, 109
White and Blue Tortilla Chili, 72–73
White Sauce, 23, 24
Wild Mushroom and Vegetable
   Gumbo with Jalapeños, 76–77
Wild Mushroom Bisque with Grilled
   Chicken, 35–36
Wontons
   Apricot, Crab, and Chile Wonton
      Soup, 120–21
   Chinese Tortilla Soup, 129
   Duck and Asian Pear Wonton Soup,
      118–19
   Lemongrass-Gingered Chicken
      Wonton Soup, 117–18
   Thai Fish Chowder with Shrimp
      Wontons, 121–22
   Wonton Pasta, 21
   Wonton Soup Broth, 17